INTERMARRIAGE:

A GUIDE FOR JEWISH PARENTS

Rabbi Robert A. Seigel
with
Debbie Herman Seigel

THE RASHI PRESS, INC.
Miami

Library of Congress Catalogue Number: 78-62678

ISBN: 0-932414-00-1

Printed in the United States of America

The Rashi Press, Inc.

Distribution Center
1882 Capri Drive
Charleston, SC 29407

ii

CONTENTS

iii

A COMMENT ON SEXISM

In the initial drafts of this book an attempt was made to neutralize the male designations of words like "his", "he", and "him". We felt that these resulted in a disruption of the flow of reading. With misgivings, the male adjectives were then placed in the text in order that the book be more easily readable.

We hope that as you read, you will understand that each male adjective refers to both male and female.

RAS & DHS

PREFACE

So. For you it's finally happened.

Somehow you thought it would always be someone else's problem.

It's not that you were unconcerned. As a parent you always were concerned and a little scared that it could happen to you. And you probably made great sacrifices to prevent it. But now it *has* happened to you.

Your child, the little baby who some day would give you beautiful Jewish grandchildren, is planning to marry a non-Jew.

"Where did I go wrong?" you ask yourself. "What can I do to prevent it?" you wonder. "Can it possibly work?"

You have become, in this perplexing age of ours, one of the new majority: the parent of an intermarried couple. Recent studies show that intermarriage now touches the lives of most American Jewish families.

Statistics on intermarriage are difficult to project. Each study uses different figures. In some studies those non-Jews who have converted to Judaism are listed among intermarried couples. In other studies only couples where there was no conversion to Judaism are counted.

Most sociologists do not differentiate between a converted Jew and a non-converted non-jew in intermarriage studies. On the other hand, however, rabbis consider a convert to be a Jew and thus exclude those couples from intermarriage statistics.

But you're not interested in sociological or religious concepts. You are interested in YOUR son or daughter and what you can do about the problem that YOU are facing.

The first thing you should know is that you are not alone. The number of Jews who marry non-Jews has reached crisis proportions. Large segments of the Jewish community are affected. In Chapter 7 we will go into some of the current statistics; but for now, you should be aware that the most conservative estimates of intermarriage in the United States is 25%. It has been suggested by several scholars that the rate has actually exceeded 50%*.

Since the beginning of the 1970's the Jewish community has been publishing articles and books about the problem. Studies have been made in Baltimore, Maryland; Boston, Massachusetts; Camden, New Jersey; Fargo, North Dakota; Kansas City, Missouri; Long Beach and Los Angeles, California; Providence, Rhode Island; and Rochester, New York. This is in addition to earlier state-wide studies in Iowa, Indiana and the District of Columbia.

---

*(25% in 1970) Sklare, Marshall. "Intermarriage and Jewish Survival." *Commentary* III 1970. p. 52.
(50% in 1973) Johnson, George E. "Comparing the Inmarried and Intermarried: Implications of the National Jewish Population Study." *Analysis.* Institute for Jewish Policy Planning and Research of the Synagogue Council of America. January 15, 1973.
(53.6% in 1973) Goldstein, Sidney. "American Jewry." *American Jewish Yearbook.* Vol. 71. New York and Philadelphia. The American Jewish Committee and the Jewish Publication Society of America. pp. 26-34. 1973.

In articles and from the pulpits the question of intermarriage has become one of the most popular subjects in the American Jewish community. It has been called the cause of the future destruction of the Jewish people. It has become a subject of great concern in the American Jewish community.

IMPLICATIONS

Let us take that 50% figure for contemporary American Jewish intermarriage. Think about it for a minute. One out of two!

Jew "A" marries another Jew.
Jew "B" marries a non-Jew.

But in the example above, we have not two, but three Jews involved. Another way of saying it more clearly is not "one out of two" but rather "two out of four":

Jew "A" marries Jew "B" in ceremony #1 (Jewish).
Jew "C" marries a non-Jew in ceremony #2 (intermarriage).
Jew "D" marries a non-Jew in ceremony #3 (intermarriage).

Thus, only one out of every three wedding ceremonies in which a Jew is wed is a Jewish/Jewish wedding. A 50% intermarriage rate actually means that 67% of "Jewish" weddings are intermarriages. TWO OUT OF THREE!

This volume is not a formula designed to wipe out intermarriage. It is not a panacea for the problems of the American Jewish community's ills. It is concerned, instead, with the very real problems that YOU are facing in the specific situation in which you find yourself.

If you are a parent, you may be experiencing this problem now. Or you may have recently gone through it. If your child isn't married yet, you know in your *kishkees* that it might happen to him. (and with the divorce rate being what it is today, **any** parent is potentially the parent of a child who may some day marry a non-Jew.)

This volume is designed to help you with the specific problem of intermarriage. It is based on years of counseling experience with couples contemplating intermarriage. During the years I served as a Hillel rabbi, I was on the "front line" of this battle. The college years are those of serious dating, mate selection, engagement and marriage. The Hillel rabbi is usually the first person to whom these couples go for advice and help. Depending upon the locale, some Hillel rabbis spend as much time counseling couples planning an intermarriage as they do with all other counseling situations combined. The reality of the problem is clear (and frightening) from the perspective of the campus worker.

The couple planning an intermarriage has need for extensive counseling. It is extremely difficult for them to cope with the problems they encounter. They and their parents experience much pain and anguish. It is a time of difficulty between parent and child. Sadly, this need not be. This guide, hopefully, will soften some of the sharpness and relieve some of the pain of this difficult time.

The first section of this book will explore the situation prior to the ceremony, when a couple has made a decision to enter into an intermarriage. We will look at some of the realities and implications of intermarriage in one's life as well as the various reactions parents might have. The realistic options before the couple will then be reviewed. Then we will trace the historical development of intermarriage from the biblical period to the present.

The second section is a discussion of the meaning of the wedding ceremony and a guideline for choosing the proper ceremony for an intermarriage.

The final section concerns conversion to Judaism as a viable alternative to intermarriage. Conversion to Judaism will be viewed historically. Then we proceed to the structure and content of a contemporary conversion program.

This is a "Parent's Guide." But in a very real sense, it is also a "Couple's Guide." Read it with an open mind, for it contains one solution I believe can work.

I

A WEDDING ON THE HORIZON

1

Should Jew and Non-Jew Marry?

The couple sitting across from me is charming. There is an aura of vitality and optimism emanating from them. One can almost visualize them as they see themselves: a lovely bride and her handsome groom who together will create a productive life. They are in love and, like most lovers, sincerely believe that "love conquers all." They are aware that there will be some problems— but nothing beyond their ability to handle. They may have financial hardships ahead; they may yet have many years of college before them. But they feel they can cope with these challenges.

However, one problem looms above all others: They do not have the parental approval they desire. For they do not share the same religion.

Having grown up in the pluralistic, secular culture of America, the young couple believes that pluralism of religion carried into their family will not detract from their feelings for each other. In some cases each is practicing his own religion. Typically, however, the non-Jew is a "former Christian" and the Jew is peripheral to Jewish observance. There are so many other factors that bind them together that they believe this one aspect of their lives (religion) surely cannot interfere with their love.

In all cases of premarital counseling, I ask many questions to determine whether the couple has thought through the potential problems they will face. I ask who will manage the budget, how many children they plan to have. I even ask how they resolve their fights. These questions often lead to further premarital counseling sessions.

But the first question I always ask is "What do you expect to get out of your marriage?" The answers are amazing. Some couples articulate mature responses that demonstrate well thought-through plans. Most couples have difficulty finding the words, but they struggle to verbalize their feelings. Even when both partners are Jewish, however, it is rare that anything Jewish is mentioned in response to the question: "What do you expect to get out of your marriage?" Most of the time, even the most prepared couples have given little thought to the Jewish nature of the home they are about to create.

In our secular society, most couples, when thinking about their marital goals, consider the question of security and companionship, of "being together," of happiness, or of having a permanent bedmate. Spiritual and religious values are seldom mentioned.

When the prospective bride and groom are both Jewish and they have answered the question without any reference to Judaism, I usually ask them if they plan to have a Jewish home. The response is normally a quick "Yes!".

"What will be Jewish about it?" I ask.

Silence descends. It takes imagination and hard thinking for them to come up with an answer which mentions a few rituals or holiday observances. And this is when they are both Jewish!

You see, even the Jew who marries another Jew shows the strain of the secular society in which we live. It is not surprising, then, to accept the reality that large numbers of young Jews grow up with Jewish identity contained somewhere under the epidermis, without their Jewishness playing a significant role in their lives. With this low profile of Judaism being common, it is not strange that many young Jews grow to maturity believing that they can create a perfect match with a non-Jew. Our couple may have heard their parents warn them against intermarriage, but they think they represent the "new generation," capable of handling that which confounded their parent's generation.

So they think.

Many couples planning to enter into an intermarriage have

4

given little thought to religion; they ignore some of the basic realities of life.

One of the first realities to face is religious involvement. More often than not, the Jewish partner completed religious education at age 13, or possibly 15. He attended synagogue services every time his parents went (in many cases, only on *Rosh Hashana* and *Yom Kippur*). Every year he went to a Passover *seder* that someone else prepared and conducted. Off at college, he discovered that he could live what seemed to be a full, fruitful life without thinking much about religious involvement or Jewish identity.

Actually, this stereotyped description could apply to all religions. Most Christian denominations experience the same sort of apathy on the part of college-aged youth. We in the Jewish community seem to feel it more sharply, however. We are a minority people, constantly aware of our obligation to maintain the faith. We are still mourning for the loss of a third of our number in the Holocaust, and fearful of additional attrition. We are greatly concerned with the prospect of the loss of even a single Jew from our community. (This attitude causes tremendous guilt to well up in the parents of any Jew who marries out of Judaism—whether or not they deserve to feel guilty.)

In later adolescence the strong ties to one's religion begin to dissipate. In the Jewish community we see this poignantly in the post-*Bar Mitzvah* Syndrome—the rebellion of the day after when the newly *"bar mitzvahed"* youngster refuses to associate voluntarily with the synagogue again. Adolescence is a time of rebellion, and religion is one of the strict disciplines to rebel against. In the late teens and early twenties Jewish observance frequently drops to the lowest possible point. For some, it reaches absolute zero.

But as the adolescent stage ends, the individual takes on responsibilities of adulthood. The former child matures. The age at maturity varies. In the Jewish community adolescence lingers longer than in most other cultures. This is due in part to the fact that Jewish youngsters are disproportionately represented in colleges and universities and have been taught to strive for graduate and post-graduate degrees. The dependency and the sometimes womb-like environment of post-graduate education often extends adolescelence to age 30!

5

THE DELAYED RELIGIOUS FACTOR

As the former child re-enters society as an adult, there is a gradual swing back toward the values once rejected. This swing is illustrated in the following chart of a person's involvement with religion as he goes through the stages of life. It is true for Jew and non-Jew alike.

CHART 1: Degree of Involvement and Identification With One's Religion at Various Ages

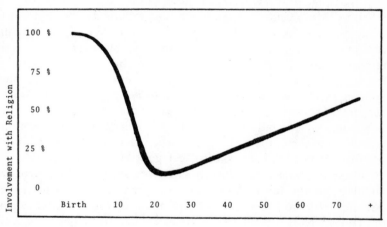

Most psychologists agree that this pattern is fairly standard for American Jews and Christians. The small child, believing every fairy tale and "white lie" told, accepts everything he knows about religion. As the child matures, some doubts about those teachings enter his mind, and finally he encounters a stage where doubts cause involvement in that religion to plunge to its lowest.

Look at the chart very carefully.

Let us now superimpose upon that chart a second chart that shows when people get married.

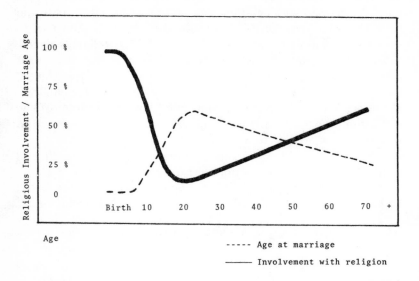

It's rather startling, isn't it? The age when most people are getting married is precisely that age when their religious involvement is at its lowest. When the couple planning to be wed claims that religion plays an insignificant role in their lives, they are probably right—for the time being.

They do not realize that as the years go by their feelings will change. If they are both of the same religion, an increasing intensity of religious identification will be yet another factor that brings them closer to each other.

But if, at the time of the wedding, they are practising (albeit casually) two different religions, then the DELAYED RELIGIOUS FACTOR can destroy everything they have built.

DELAYED RELIGIOUS FACTOR: AN EXAMPLE

One Saturday afternoon several years ago a middle aged man came into my study at the temple shortly after we had concluded the *Shabbat* service. I had never met him before. He was obviously distressed, and in a few minutes poured forth his tale with tears of rage. Some years before, when he married a Roman Catholic girl, he hadn't really cared much for his own Jewish background. It had been no great problem for him to make a vow that any children they would have would be raised as Catholics. The couple had been blessed with children, and that Saturday morning would have been his eldest son's *bar mitzvah*—had that son been Jewish.

It took almost fifteen years for the Delayed Religious Factor to strike that couple, but its force was volcanic. He was distraught and had been unable to sleep for the past few nights. He resented his wife and broke into tears whenever he spoke of his children. He did not want to go back home; for him the trauma of the realization of what he had given up was overwhelming. He saw no way for his marriage to survive.

As best I could, I tried to give him the spiritual uplift and comfort he was seeking. I struggled for words and fought back my own tears as I cried inside for his agony. When he left my study, he had put aside his suicidal thought. But he left a broken man.

BUILDING A LASTING FOUNDATION

In these days of Zero Population Growth, some couples planning to marry have decided not to have children at all. But no young couple can know for certain at the time of their marriage that they definitely will not have children. Even in this day and age, unplanned pregnancies do occur, and once pregnant, the couple might very well decide to become parents. Or, a few years down the road, a couple who had decided not to have children might change their minds. And with enlightened attitudes toward adoption, physical inability does not limit parenthood. Thus, the issue of children must be a part of the discussion of the future for any young couple—especially a couple involving itself in an intermarriage.

Children need strong, positive role models in order to become emotionally mature and productive adults. They need mothers and fathers who know themselves and practice their beliefs with the conviction and security that can only come in a unified home.

Being a Jew, for example, gives your child a set of beliefs and values to see him through the challenges of a lifetime. Judaism gives a sense of history that includes and transcends the history of the individual family. It gives a sense of belonging to a people with a four thousand year recorded history; it gives one an extended family encompassing the entire globe. Being a Jew gives one a sense of knowing who one is and how he fits into the scheme of things. (So, too, of course, a child raised in a richly dedicated Christian home.)

People need rituals, too, as tangible symbols of the abstract concepts that underlie them. As a Hillel director I counseled with many students who grew up in homes where more than one religion was practiced. These students were suffering with confusion and extended identity crisis. They expressed their feelings, their anger, and their pain. The hostility would come out in violent spasms: "My parents robbed me!" "I want to be a part of the Jewish community, but I'm afraid." "I'm ashamed that I don't know anything about my own religion." "Tell me, Rabbi, am I a Jew?" Each and every one of them was asking the same question: "Who am I?"

These young people are candidates for academic degrees, some on graduate level. But they still struggle with the very basic question of identity.

This is not, of course, an uncommon question. In fact, it is one that every maturing young person should be asking. The problem is that for young people who grew up in a home with more than one religion (or no religion) they have no point of reference, no focus, no basis upon which to structure the search.

A popular entertainer some years ago, boasting about his own intermarriage, said that of their four children, they were raising "one as a Jew, one as a Christian, a third is being taught both Judaism and Christianity, while the fourth is being exposed neither to Judaism nor Christianity." This may relieve the entertainer and his wife from their own problem; but what about the problems they are creating for their children? Brothers and sisters who celebrate different holidays, who worship differently, who do not share the same values, rituals, symbols, calendar, language and heritage must surely grow to adulthood without the feeling of unity that ties a family together.

Someone superficially knowledgeable of Judaism and Christianity might think that the value system of both great religions is the same. Although they stem from a common root and both are based on ethical systems, there are many values that the two do not share.

> Christians are taught to love their fellowmen. In Judaism we are taught not how to **feel** about another, but rather, how to **treat** another.

9

In Judaism, the body, made in the image of God, is sacred. According to Jewish law we cannot mar the body (e.g. tatoos, pierced ears, etc. are forbidden) and are religiously obligated to protect our physical health. In fact, we are prohibited from living in a community without a physician!

A corollary to this is *kashrut*, the kosher dietary laws. In Judaism, it is considered to be most noble to be a vegetarian, but since most of us cannot adjust to that, we are forbidden from eating any meat that has been killed in a way that causes pain or that is done for pleasure (hunting is forbidden) or from an animal that has been mistreated.

Our bodies are sacred. What goes into them is important, and the very act of eating is ritual-laden in Judaism to constantly remind us of this.

One of the most basic philosophic concepts in life is the nature of man. The Christian view, based on the concept of "original sin," is the antithesis of Judaism's emphasis on the good qualities of human nature.

Unlike the traditional Christian view that the highest form of sex is no sex (eg. virgin birth, celibacy), in Judaism we see sex as given by God, a beautiful natural phenomenon. To the Jew, one who does not marry and have children is not fulfilling his religious obligations.

We could go on for pages just listing the various differences between Christian and Jewish values. To say they are different is not to say that one is automatically superior to the other. They are different and at times are in conflict. A Jewish physician, for example, faced with saving a pregnant woman or her unborn child, would opt to save the mother. While on the other hand, a Christian physician might well be more concerned for the unborn child who has not had a chance to be "saved." When values clash in a home environment, even in apparently subtle ways, the unity of the family is challenged.

Some couples honestly believe that they can expose their children to both religions—the religion of the father and the religion of the mother—and when the child is older, the child will decide for himself. This is absurd.

If the child chooses anything, it will be neither Judaism nor Christianity. There will be too much confusion to sort out one of the two authentic religions. In all likelihood it will be an amalgam of both religions. Judaism will lose; the child will not be fully

Jewish. Christianity will lose; the child will not be fully Christian. The child himself will lose; having created his own hybrid religion, he will find himself without the fellowship of others who share that uniqueness with him.

But most importantly, teaching both religions to the child, teaching two sets of values and two sets of rituals, and letting him decide later, just doesn't work. The resulting confusion will prevent him from seeing the true beauty of either religion. Cultural pluralism can be "broadening" only when one has a firm foundation, a positive self-identification upon which to base cultural comparisons.

THE QUESTION OF CHILDREN

Why do people have children? Why did you have children?

We are used to answering that sort of question with lofty reasons: perpetuation of humanity, fruit of love, the desire to give of oneself, etc. But psychologically, at the core of human instinct, we have children for one basic reason: to perpetuate ourselves, to create little "me's." We really want our children to be like us. We *kvell* whenever our child voluntarily accepts our own values or "walks in our footsteps."

Cutting through the outer defenses, we must admit that we have children so that they can perpetuate our selves, our values, our beliefs, our standards. If we didn't care, if we really didn't care how our children developed, we would teach them "Thou shalt not steal" while at the same time also teaching them "How to steal without getting caught." Then, when the child was older, he could mull over both of the teachings to which he was exposed and decide which to live by.

It sounds foolish, doesn't it? Not really. The parent who exposes his children to two different religious identities, expecting that child to choose one later in life, is doing percisely this. Judaism is not Christianity, and Christianity is not Judaism. They are two great religions, but they are not the same. They differ on holidays, rituals, symbols, beliefs, histories, cultures, calenders, languages, and attitudes toward life. Exposing a child to both religions as the child's primary religion is a surefire way to pre-plan a later identity crisis.

When parents come from different religious backgrounds and

enter the marriage with those separate identities, many problems ensue. Letting children decide their own religion is irresponsible. The responsible parent has an obligation to teach the values and identification he feels the child should have. Some intermarried couples realize this and are able to avoid a few of the many problems they are creating by making a decision for their children. This is no different from the major decisions that all parents make for their children, except that in the case of intermarriage, one can usually expect the Delayed Religious Factor to give the marriage a "whammy" of a shock in later years.

There are intermarried couples who decide before marriage what religion their child will have. But other couples do not; they procrastinate, they avoid confronting the issue.

A TRAGIC EXAMPLE

There was a lovely couple. He was Protestant and she was Jewish. Neither really cared too much for religious labels when they were wed, but both were unwilling to convert to the other's religion. They figured that if they had children, they would decide upon the children's religious upbringing later. It seemed to be a good solution for them. They were happy and satisfied with their relationship. But, unfortunately, they were unaware of the Delayed Religious Factor.

They were blessed with children, two beautiful daughters. When the elder was five years of age, they felt it was time to make the decision about their children's religious education. They were prepared to send the older child to religious school, but they weren't sure which kind of religious education to give her. So, they went "shopping." They checked out the local synagogue and the local church. But they were unable to make a speedy decision.

Then, suddenly, one of the girls died.

It was a tragedy. Wherever a child dies, there is only pain. But this was an occasion that I will never forget.

At the side of the bed, as the child literally breathed her last breath, instead of grieving together, her parents were fighting. They were arguing over who was going to bury her, the minister or the rabbi.

They had thought there was time to make a decision about religious identity, and they were caught unprepared at a time when they were most vulnerable.

12

It didn't have to be. They could have avoided the ugliness that neither of them should have been forced to face at such a horrible time. When they were married they thought that postponing a decision about their children's religion was a way of resolving the problem. And they learned too late that postponing this critical problem did not resolve it. A couple that cannot resolve this kind of problem before marriage will find it no easier, and, in all likelihood, far more difficult, to resolve after marriage.

Marriage, even under the best conditions, is difficult. It is a process of working, constantly working, to build a lasting relationship. Every barrier placed between husband and wife make the success of that marriage more difficult. Religious difference in marriage is one of the most serious barriers that a couple can place between themselves. If they are truly in love and desire to mold a unified life, it will be difficult enough with one religion. The increased divorce rate testifies to that. But when they enter matrimony with two separate religions, they are playing Russian roulette with their future.

2

The Parental Response

The most difficult problem which faces intermarrying couples is the reaction of the Jewish parents. The most intelligent, successful people are often reduced to hysterical, vindictive, irrational actions when they realize their child is going to marry a non-Jew.

Is this reaction understandable? Very much so. It is as if the ghosts of all past generations fall upon their shoulders with overwhelming weight. The dreaded nightmare has actually happened to them.

THE RELAY RACE

Picture, if you will, a relay race. This is a race where the runners carry, not a stick, but a lighted candle. When each runner crosses the finish line, he gives the candle to the next runner. As long as the candle stays lit, the team continues to run.

This race has been going on for 4,000 years, and many runners have suffered greatly in order to bring that candle to the finish line and pass it on. Now, your child is completing his lap. But he stops short of the finish line; he blows out the candle. He destroys all that the previous runners have accomplished. You, his parent, look into the faces of all those who preceded him. You feel shame. You feel defeat, You feel that you have failed.

15

Indeed, it is easy to understand the violent reactions of many Jewish parents in such a situation. But does this reaction do any good? And what can result from this outburst of anger?

ARE YOU ASHAMED?

At the core of the parent's feeling is the belief that "I have failed." For some parents, this is true. Some parents have not given their children a good Jewish education and provided proper role models as committed Jews. These parents **have** failed in their responsibility to raise Jewish children. But this is not the case in most instances of intermarriage. Intermarriage can happen **despite** everything the parent has done.

According to traditional Jewish law, when a child is small, whatever sins he commits are "charged" to the parents. On *Yom Kippur,* for example, the parents stand before God accused of whatever wrongdoings their child has committed. But after age thirteen, the child can no longer sluff off his inadequacies onto his parents. The thirteen year old must attend *Yom Kippur* services, must fast, and must stand—alone—before God to answer for his own actions.

The parent who voluntarily accepts the "guilt" of his child's real or assumed misdeeds after age thirteen is doing so unnecessarily. Many parents do just this because they have trained themselves to be reflected in their child's actions.

You may have pushed your child into an education; and when he achieves his ultimate acclaim and success, you *kvell* because you feel deep down inside that you share his success.

From the first "A" on a report card through every achievement of his life, you thrilled each time as if you yourself had accomplished the feat. Yes, you may have helped inspire and prod; but your child did the work. Your child deserves the credit.

Likewise, when a child errs—after age thirteen—he alone stands responsible.

When your child intermarries, you have not failed. If you can remove the guilt that YOU have placed upon yourself, you will be able to deal rationally with this problem. If you become crippled from self-imposed guilt, you can only make the situation even worse than it already is.

How, then, should you react?

Reaction #1: Rejection of Intermarriage

Some parents have become so upset with the prospect of their child marrying out of Judaism that they sit *shiva* and pronounce the child dead. Others throw the child out of the house. Others cut off financial aid. Others forbid the child from bringing the intended spouse into their home. As one parent put it to her daughter, "Don't you dare bring that—that—that THING into my house!" This reaction frequently allows the parent to vent his feelings, to express his anger and frustrations. But what else does it accomplish?

In most cases it accomplishes the exact opposite of what the parent wants. The child, rejected by his own parents, turns to his intended spouse with increased intensity. Perhaps the couple has been considering marriage at some time in the vague future. Perhaps in the months ahead they will decide (for many possible reasons) not to marry. But when separated from wise and reasoned parental counsel by the barrier of rejection, the child may well feel the need to defend the non-Jewish partner who has been "attacked" by the parent, and rush directly into an early marriage.

The parent who rejects his child pushes him right into marriage! I have seen many young people who felt forced into a marriage for which they were not ready because parents had cut off financial and moral support.

Actually, the rejecting parent is the strongest ally that intermarriage has.

WHAT IF THE NON-JEW CONVERTS?

One might expect that the Jewish parent's rejection of the marriage would be washed away if the non-Jew converted to Judaism. Sadly, this is seldom the case. A most ironic tragedy is the situation where the non-Jew undergoes conversion, becomes a Jew, and is **still** rejected by the Jewish parents. In a later chapter we will discuss this issue. But for now, let us state that rejecting a child who plans to marry a convert to Judaism normally results in:

(1) An earlier marriage, and/or

(2) The Jewish child marrying a non-Jew instead of a convert to Judaism.

17

The process of conversion is often as hard on the Jewish spouse-to-be as it is on the convert. When the Jewish parents heap rejection on top of this hardship, the Jewish child sometimes feels such anger at his parents that it becomes hatred of Judaism. When this happens, the Jewish partner frequently pressures the conversion student to cease his studies and remain a non-Jew. "If they won't accept her as a Jew," the child reasons, "why should she bother?" Thus, the rejected child marries a non-Jew whereas previously he had intended to marry a (converted) Jew.

Parental rejection, then, results in both the parents and the children having an opportunity to unleash all their deeply felt hostilities. Both feel righteous. Each has stood on principle. But the parents have lost a child. And the child has lost his parents. And the Jewish people has lost another link in the chain of our heritage.

Reaction #2: Approval of Intermarriage

Sometimes parents wholeheartedly welcome an intermarriage. It doesn't happen often, but it does occur. The Jewish child announces his intent to marry a non-Jew. The parent, who knows and likes the intended spouse, is happy. For that parent, intermarriage is the way of the future. He sees nothing wrong with it. He gives his blessing to the union.

This, fortunately, is not the manner of most Jewish parents. For if it were, it would signal the end of Judaism and the Jewish people.

Reaction #3: The Middle Road

If accepting and rejoicing in the proposed marriage is an affront to Jewish identity, and rejecting the intermarriage only makes the situation worse, what **can** a parent do?

There **is** a middle road, a sensible path that a parent can take. In order to travel this road, the Jewish parent needs to pack the proper baggage. He needs to take along his rationality and reason. He should pack a lot of love and understanding as well. He ought to leave behind vindictiveness, guilt and anger.

In order to take the first step on this road, the parent must understand the distinction between ACCEPTANCE and AP-PROVAL. To approve an act is to give your blessings to it. Ap-

18

proval implies that the act is proper and good. Acceptance, however, does not imply that the act is proper. Acceptance is simply admitting the existence of something and recognizing the need to coexist with it.

The parent should carefully explain to the child the distinction between these two responses, acceptance and approval. When a parent disapproves of any action of his child, he does not automatically reject the child. On the contrary, a loving parent **often** criticizes (disapproves) the actions of his child while letting the child know that he is loved (accepted). When your child plans to intermarry and you disapprove of his doing so, your most effective approach is to:

(1) Let your child know that you accept him; regardless of what he might ever do, this will always be your child and you will always love him.

(2) Inform your child that if it is his determination to marry a non-Jew, you will accept the reality of the situation. You will not turn your back on him.

Only then will you be in a position to say the next part. Only then will you have set the ground rules of trust and love so that you can speak emotionally but rationally, and your child can hear what you are saying. Then you can explain to him that you do not approve of the marriage—and why. You can offer reasons why intermarriage can be harmful to him.

(3) But you must end up by reiterating that although you disapprove of this intermarriage, you will accept it.

By taking this position, you will keep open the opportunity to communicate with your child at least on the level that existed before this situation arose. In time the young couple may decide not to wed. They might decide that the non-Jew should convert and remove the stigma of intermarriage.

But even if your child persists and enters an intermarriage, you will be better off. Judaism will have lost, granted. But you will not have lost a child; nor he a parent.

You might say to your child, "I do not approve of your wedding plans, and I think you are doing something very wrong. But I will be there with you, because whatever you do, you will always be my child." If it is a non-Jewish wedding ceremony, you do not have to participate (you do not have to walk down the aisle), *but you should be in attendance.* Not attending your child's wedding, regardless of the circumstances, will sever most bridges to a later reconciliation, even when the parent and child previously had a close relationship.

"...HOW DO I SHOW MY FACE IN PUBLIC?"

Your child is marrying a non-Jew in a non-Jewish wedding ceremony. You can muster up the strength to attend the ceremony. But what about the side effects?

"Should I send out invitations?

"How should I tell my friends?"

"Is there some way we can conceal that it is an intermarriage?"

These are real questions for a parent who disapproves of intermarriage. It is legitimate to be concerned about them. Unfortunately, however, some parents avoid the basic issue of their child's intermarriage by expressing hostility at their child. This does not resolve the problem.

Should you send out invitations? How should you tell your friends? The reality level of these questions is: "Can I acknowledge the fact that this is actually happening?" You must decide for yourself whether or not to send invitations, for this is truly your option. But as far as telling friends, you have no option. Your friends will eventually learn of the marriage, and you will be embarrassed when they congratulate you. Tell them first. Your child is, after, all, getting married. It is a significant event in his life, as well as yours. Sure, you had hoped and prayed that the marriage would be to a Jew; but when it is a marriage to a non-Jew, **it is still your child's wedding.** You may be saddened by your child's decision and deeply disapprove of his act. Okay; it is legitimate to feel sad, to feel a sense of loss, to feel disappointed. But it is not legitimate to feel guilty or ashamed.

If your child intermarries, accept the reality, tell your friends as you would for any major event in your life. Do not sit *shiva* or cut your child out of your will. Attend the wedding and pray that somehow your child will escape the many pitfalls on the path he has chosen.

3

The Couple's Options

A couple facing an intermarriage has several options:

(1) Both can leave their religions and find some "neutral" third religion.
(2) They can give up both their religions and have no religion.
(3) They can attempt to retain both religions in their marriage.
(4) The Jew can convert to Christianity.
(5) The non-Jew can convert to Judaism.

Let us look at each of these possibilities.

(1) FINDING A THIRD RELIGION

When the religious attachment of neither bride nor groom is strong, this option seems tempting. For the sake of creating a marriage where there will be unity of religion, some couples reject both of their former religions, and instead they adopt a third, neutral one. Most commonly this neutral religion is Unitarianism/Universalism or the Society of Friends (Quakers). (In fact, this practice has given rise to the joke wherein the Quaker leader says, "Some of my best Friends are Jews.")

Finding a third religion seems like a viable option in that it responds immediately to the problem facing the couple. It instantly transforms an intermarriage into a marriage with a unified religion. But the decision has problems of its own.

Neither set of parents will find joy in this option. For the Jewish parents, it means their grandchildren will not be Jewish.

It means fully giving up one's former religion with all its cultural and historical attachments. It means finding NOT the best, most ideal religion for the couple, but one which offers so little that there are few rituals or beliefs to alienate either of them.

It is a compromise that falls far short of the ideal and meets few on-going spiritual, cultural or social needs of the parties involved. The nature of a compromise is that neither partner really has his way; neither partner fully retains the religious identity of his past.

If one can so readily shed his identity, you might ask, then why not have one of the partners convert to the other's religions in the first place?

(2) GIVING UP RELIGION

Of course, in a secular society such as ours, it is always possible for both partners to give up their religions and settle on having no religion in their home. For some few couples, this works. But for most, it does not meet their needs.

In later years, as the Delayed Religious Factor comes into play, one or both of the partners will find himself longing for a return to religion. When this happens, the neutral household becomes a "delayed intermarriage." What started out as a harmonious and unified (albeit religionless) home erupts into a divided and unhappy family.

When the couple has children they soon learn that values, ethics and morals are extremely difficult to teach without the concrete symbols of religion. The ideal of freedom, for example, can be quite difficult for a young child to understand; yet the holiday of Passover personalizes the concept through ritual. The need to be thankful for what we have is easily taught to children through the rituals of *Sukkot*. The struggle between idolatry and the one God is understood by children celebrating *Chanuka*. From the holiday of *Tu Bishvat* we learn the need and importance of conservation. The Sabbath candles and wine allow the youngster to relate to the concepts of *Shabbat*—of light and sweetness and joy. Within a Christian context, the child learns the concept of Messianic fulfillment through the holiday and rituals of Christmas. And Easter rituals teach the complex theology of salvation.

The need to give one's child a moral and ethical base as well as a cultural and social environment often forces parents to seek out organized religion. So, again, they have only delayed the decision.

(3) BOTH RELIGIONS TOGETHER

Some couples opt to retain both of their separate religions, creating a home atmosphere that might be called "gemixte gepickles." Both religions are observed, and the couple tries to make a go of it. Formerly, Roman Catholics who married out of their faith were excommunicated. But in our contemporary world, Protestants, Catholics and Jews can find churches and temples that will accept them when their spouses are not of the same faith. But this is an intermarriage, and all of the warnings of Chapter 1 come into play in such a situation.

A loving Christian wife, for example, might look upon her Jewish husband's attempt to observe *Shabbat* on the same level as when he goes out one night a week "with the boys." The person of the other religion can **observe** but can never **share** the religious rituals and holidays of his mate. To illustrate:

(a) The Jewish mate wants to observe *Shabbat;* the non-Jewish mate wants to go shopping that Saturday afternoon. The non-Jew says, from his perspective, "I went to services with you last night, and you went with me to church last Sunday. What's this all-day Saturday thing? It's unfair."

(b) The non-Jewish mate might well say to the partner prior to Passover, "You want ME to clean out all the bread in the house? YOU do it!"

(c) With many Jews returning to religious rituals, it is not uncommon for one to observe the kosher dietary laws after several years of non-observance. Can you imagine the non-Jewish mate's reaction? "I'll be damned if I'll give up my bacon for breakfast!"

(d) Or picture a home with a portrait of Jesus on a wall with a candle burning under it. What goes through the Jewish mate's mind

23

when he lights the *Yizkor* candle for his parents on the other side of the room? One ritual diminishes the meaning of the other.

(e) In America, even in areas of high Jewish concentration, we are a minority. This is especially felt during the Christmas season. The Jewish home is one of the few bastions to which a Jew can flee to escape the endless Christmas carols and decorations and greetings. If one of the partners in the home celebrates Christmas as a religious event, there is no sanctuary for the Jew.

(f) And what about the Jew who fasts on *Yom Kippur* coming home to a house with music playing and the aroma of cooking food in the air?

(g) The breakdown of communication between husband and wife can be most serious during those times when Israel is in peril. The non-Jew, try as he might, cannot fully understand the raw fear and anxiety of the Jewish mate.

Be careful of such situations! You should be aware that a home which has two religions in reality has neither. A home where Christianity and Judaism are both practiced is neither Jewish nor Christian. A *mezuzah* on the door does not neutralize the Christmas tree. In such a home both religions lose.

For a home to be Jewish, it must be peopled with Jews. To be Jewish a home must be a sanctuary, a place of Jewish worship. The home is the primary religious setting of Judaism. The focus of family life and holidays revolve around the home: *Kashrut,* the Passover *seder,* lighting the *Chanuka* lights, the *Shabbat* meals.

Attempting to allow two religions to co-exist in one home creates divisiveness, not cohesion. Marriage is difficult enough without religion being another factor to separate the family.

(4) THE JEW CAN CONVERT TO CHRISTIANITY

Occasionally this happens, but very rarely. Recognizing the need to create one unified religion in the home, one possibility is for the Jewish partner to give up his Judaism and become a Christian. It happens rarely because in order for a Jew to become a Christian, he must:

(a) Accept a body of theology and beliefs that are alien to him, and

(b) Give up the culture of the Jewish people which usually has deep psychological roots.

Most Jews, even those who proudly assert that they are not religious, are incapable of becoming sincere converts to Christianity. There are just too many barriers. Greatest among them is the accepting of Jesus as the central personality of one's life.

Usually when I am counseling a couple contemplating intermarriage and the Jewish partner has stated that Judaism holds little meaning for him, I use a special technique. During our conversation—at a point when it is least expected—I turn to the Jewish partner and say, "You should convert to Christianity!"

It always works. The Jewish partner immediately goes on the defensive and rattles off a whole list of reasons why he cannot give up his Jewish identity. I just sit back and listen. I don't have to tell him why he should remain a Jew. **He** does it himself. Of course, behind this ploy is the reasoning that anyone who really might seriously consider becoming a Christian wouldn't be sitting in a rabbi's study discussing an impending marriage. In most cases, whether he knows it or not, the Jewish partner is desperately trying to find some way of remaining Jewish while marrying a non-Jew. The idea of converting to Christianity is seldom given much thought.

(5) THE CHRISTIAN CAN CONVERT TO JUDAISM

According to traditional Jewish law, once a convert has become a Jew, that person is a full, first-class Jew. No one is even allowed to refer to him as a convert. Conversion to Judaism is legitimate. (For more on this, see Chapter 7).

In order for a Christian to convert to Judaism, the Jewish spouse must be prepared to give much support, time and energy. Many rabbis insist that the Jewish partner go through the entire process along with the intended spouse. It creates another bond of cohesion to bring the couple even closer together. It also enables the conversion student to share the reactions of the born Jew along every step of the way. And, as I tell my students, "We don't want the convert to live with a born Jew who knows less about Judaism than he does."

When a Jewish child informs his parents that he is planning to marry someone who is converting to Judaism, the parents usually react negatively. Ironically, the convert's Christian parents—who have real reason to feel rejected—usually accept the decision of their child, and they learn to live with it. On the other hand, however, the Jewish parents—whose child has not rejected them—usually react with anger and hostility. They ignore the fact that Jewish law condones conversion to Judaism. They forget love between parent and child. They neglect their own rationality.

Many Jewish parents whose child is planning to marry a convert act in a most irrational and destructive manner. Much of the counseling the convert receives during the course of his conversion process focuses on how to break through the barrier that the Jewish parents have erected. In this situation, it is the parents—not the child—who are acting improperly. And in time, most of these parents come to realize that the convert *is* a Jew and that their grandchildren will be Jewish.

A WORD TO THE COUPLE

If **you** are the person planning to marry a non-Jew who is converting to Judaism, you can expect a negative reaction from your parents. No matter how difficult it becomes, there is one thing you should **not** do. You should not respond back in anger. In time the problem will be resolved, but the more hostility that comes to the fore, the more difficult will be the process of healing the wounds later.

You will certainly be hurt by your parent's reactions. They may threaten. They may call both of you names. They may "lay a guilt trip" on you. You may be sorely tempted to respond back in anger. You have been hurt. But with the passing of time the wounds will begin to heal. In time your parents will come to accept your partner as a Jew. There will be need to reestablish the family closeness that once was.

If your parents have been hostile to you, reconciliation will be difficult but attainable. If you, too, said ugly things, the road back will be long and painful.

BECOMING A JEW

A Christian can convert to Judaism much more easily than a Jew can convert to Christianity. A former Christian needs to give up one central doctrine: his belief in Jesus as a special person. Most of the other bodies of theology can easily be transferred from the one religion to the other. The cultural aspects of Judaism can be learned. Judaism is a religion of "doing."

> The *Talmud* tells us that when we die and approach heaven, we will not be asked if we believed in God. We will be asked what we did with our lives.

> The *Midrash* has God saying the following: "I would be content if My people did not believe in Me—if only they observed My laws!"

We are a people of *mitzvot,* of laws and deeds; and it is much easier to accept guidelines to living than mandates to belief. We are not faith-oriented. The faith is there, but it is an undercurrent that weaves throughout the pattern of living. If belief and action come into conflict, belief becomes secondary. For example, let us take the illustration of a bigot, one who hates a certain group of people because of their race or religion or what-have-you. For the sake of illustration we will call these "objects of prejudice" the "OOPS."

A faith-centered religion would tell the bigot to change his attitudes and feelings, to try to love the OOPS, to believe that they are the same as he. But this is difficult. Prejudice, or any learned belief, is slow to change. And if the bigot was ultimately unable to lose his hostility of the OOPS, he would always carry with him the guilt imposed by his religion for failure to believe.

An action-centered religion like Judaism, on the other hand, would not emphasize the level of belief and feeling. Judaism would tell the bigot that even if he persists in hating OOPS, he must **treat** them exactly as he treats all other people. Acknowledging the lengthy process of forcing a change of belief upon a person, Judaism instead forces a change of what one actually does. There seems to be a good psychological basis for this. If the bigot is forced to live with OOPS and treat them in every respect the same as non-OOPS, in time he will come to believe and know that OOPS and non-OOPS are really equal. Believing one thing and living the opposite will force either the belief or the action to change, and since Judaism demands the acting out *(mitzvah/*deed system), the belief must ultimately change.

Most non-Jews, however, who find themselves in an intermarriage situation are really not practicing Christians. Most have already rejected their religious upbringing and are amenable to the suggestion that they explore the possibility of becoming Jewish. Frequently, all it takes is a little encouragement from the Jewish partner and some understanding from the parents.

TIMING OF THE DECISION

Whatever decision the couple makes regarding their future religious identity, it is vital that they make it **before** the wedding. Some couples, coerced by both sets of parents, pressured by friends, hassled by all the details involved in the actual wedding plans, choose to postpone the decision until after they are married. After all, they are in love. They respect each other. They know that they will be able to work it out.

No! If they cannot resolve this problem before getting married, the odds are against their ability to do it later.

If you fear that the problem is so acute that forcing the issue prior to the wedding might break apart the couple, remember that resolving the religious question will be more difficult after the wedding. The problem will remain; but after they are married, they will either be forced to accept something they dislike—or get divorced.

The religious life of the family is a major issue. IF THE COUPLE CANNOT DECIDE BEFORE THE CEREMONY, THEY ARE NOT READY FOR MARRIAGE.

4

You Are Not Alone

Sometimes it is believed that intermarriage is a new phenonomenon. When Jews and non-Jews desire to marry each other these days it is frequently viewed as caused by the pressures of American secular society. "In Europe we didn't have this problem!" comes the lament.

True. In Europe Jews were often prevented from engaging in business with non-Jews, much less marrying them. The wall of social separation ran both ways. In William Shakespeare's *The Merchant of Venice,* which portrayed common life between Jew and non-Jew in the late Sixteenth—early Seventeenth Century, the limits of interaction between Jew and gentile are sharply presented as Shylock, the Jew, declines a social invitation from Bassanio, the gentile:

I will not eat with you, drink with you, pray with you.
—Act I, Scene 3

In this subtle way, Shakespeare was expressing the common sentiment of the society at that time: a hardened wall of social, cultural and religious separation between the two communities. Obviously intermarriage was not possible within the ghetto walls or within the Pale of Settlement.

But ghettos did not always exist. There **were** times when Jews and non-Jews intermingled. What happened then? Did intermarriages take place? Were they common? Were they successful? How did the Jewish community view them? To find the answer we must go back, starting at the earliest source, the Bible.

THE BIBLICAL PERIOD

In the early part of the Bible, during the pre-Exilic period (before the Babylonian Exile of 586 B.C.E.), there were no clearcut prohibitions against Jews marrying non-Jews. There were, of course, those who spoke out against intermarriage—but they spoke without the backing of a definitive law.

Remember the story of Abraham's sending his servant back to the homeland to find a wife for his son, Isaac? Abraham commanded the servant not to take a wife for Isaac from "the daughters of the Canaanites among whom I dwell." Sounds like a modern day parent? But just a few generations (and a few chapters) later, Joseph married a non-Jew, Asenath, the daughter of Potiperah, Priest of Or. Although Abraham very clearly wanted to set the standard of marrying within the Jewish people, only three generations later intermarriage was a reality.

And how about Moses, the Lawgiver? Each Jewish bride and groom recite the central oath in the wedding ceremony which translates literally as "according to the Law of Moses." Yet, Moses himself married Zipporah, a non-Jew (the daughter of the priest of Midian).

How about David? Yes, the great Kind David, from whose lineage will some day arise the Messiah, married non-Jews: Bathsheba, a Hittite, and Maacah, from Geshur.

Then, again, there was Samson who married the Phillistine Delilah—against his parents' wishes. And we all know what happened to him!

King Ahab of Judah was wed to Jezabel, a Zidonian worshipper of Baal.

Perhaps the two most famous cases of intermarriage in biblical history are well known today because Jewish holidays have been created around the personalities involved. But even more telling, these holidays might never have been, had the intermarriages not taken place.

The first is about a Jewish girl by the name of Hadassah who wanted so badly to marry the non-Jewish King of Persia that she concealed her Jewish identity and changed her name to Esther.— And every *Purim* we give thanks that Queen Esther was able to intercede with her non-Jewish husband to prevent the destruction of the Jewish people.

The second is Ruth, a Moabite, who married a Jew, and later—following his death—converted to Judaism. The Book of Ruth is read every year at *Shavuot,* the festival of accepting the Law; for in our tradition nothing symbolizes acceptance of the Law in such a profound way as Ruth's life. Remember what she said to Naomi, her mother-in-law?

> Entreat me not to leave thee, and to return from following after thee; for whither thou goest, I will go; and where thou lodgest, I will lodge; thy people shall be my people, and thy God my God . . .
> —Ruth I:16

During the biblical period, in times of peace and tranquility, intermarriage **was** common.

The slowly growing movement against intermarriage surfaced primarily in times of national crisis, only to recede again until the next crisis. The major periods of opposition to intermarriage were:

(1) **The Deuteronomic Reformation** of 685 B.C.E. when a whole series of laws were imposed on the people in one fell swoop.

(2) **The end of the Babylonian Exile** in 536 B.C.E. when the Jews, returning to the land of Israel, found Jerusalem destroyed and the nation in shambles.

(3) **The rule of the Hasmoneans** in the Second Century B.C.E. during which time cruel and harsh edicts were enacted.

(4) **The Roman Wars** of the First and Second Centuries C.E. when the Jewish nation underwent its death pangs under the heels of the Roman legions.

The earliest injunction against intermarriage can be found in Exodus 34:16. When the Israelites were promised the land of

Israel, they were enjoined by God to destroy the seven resident nations (the Hittites, Girgashites, Amorites, Canaanites, Perizzites, Hivites and Jebusites). One of the reasons stated for this mass annihilation of the Seven Nations was to prevent intermarriage.

> When the Lord thy God shall bring thee into the land whither thou goest to possess it, and shall cast out many nations before thee, the Hittite, and the Girgashite, and the Amorite, and the Canaanite, and the Perizzite, and the Hivite, and the Jebusite, seven nations greater and mightier than thou; and when the Lord thy God shall deliver them up before thee, and thou shalt smite them; then thou shalt utterly destroy them; thou shalt make no covenant with them, nor show mercy unto them; *neither shalt thou make marriages with them:* thy daughter thou shalt not give unto his son, nor his daughter shalt thou take unto thy son. For he will turn away thy son from following Me, that they may serve other gods . . .
>
> —Deuteronomy 7:1-4

This is a passage from the period of the Deuteronomic Reformation, clearly spelling out a prohibition against marrying idolaters. Later, in the Talmudic period, the Rabbis argued over the word "them" in the phrase "neither shalt thou make marriages with **them.**" Some argued that it referred only to the Seven Nations spelled out in the original prohibition; but a majority view held that it represented a general prohibition against marriage with any non-Jew. *(Talmud Avoda Zara 36B* and *Yebamot 77A)* From that time on, the original statement against the seven nationalities became a universal prohibition.

Some opposition to intermarriage always existed in all periods of Jewish history, although the practice continued in day-to-day life. In biblical times, like today, although the authorities upheld strict rules against intermarriage, the people somehow found ways of circumventing the law. Jewish and non-Jewish young men and women have mixed socially and intermarried since the earliest days of the Jewish people.

King Solomon, who collected wives as some people collect postage stamps, was married to several non-Jewish women simultaneously. He was wed to an Egyptian, to some Moabites, Ammonites, Edomites, Zidonians and Hittites. Interestingly, some of his wives were from the prohibited Seven Nations. Public opposition to his marriage to non-Jews began to surface, but it is uncertain whether the hostility was due to his having wed non-Jews in general or specifically women of the Seven Nations.

The harshest statements against intermarriage during the biblical period came during the end of the Babylonian Exile when the people were attempting to rebuild the Temple and the nation. The Prophet Malachai clearly opposed any intermarriage at all. And Ezra the Scribe, leader of the post-Exilic period, actually went a giant step further. Ezra not only disapproved of Jews marrying non-Jews, he demanded that all Jewish men who were wed to non-Jewish women immediately divorce them. He had the support of the prophet/politician Nehemiah.

THE POST-BIBLICAL PERIOD

Up until the year 70 C.E., when the Second Temple fell, there were always conflicting and opposing views on all subjects, including intermarriage. But the Romans put an end to that. With the Roman destruction of the ruling Saducees, the Pharisaic party was left alone with the power of authority in the Jewish community. And with this awesome authority falling into the hands of one single party, many clear-cut laws were enacted.

One of the first acts of the Pharisees following the destruction of the Second Temple was to interpret biblical law so that intermarriage was understood as a violation of basic Jewish law.

Up until that time individuals had spoken out against intermarriage, but no one could officially prevent it. With this new interpretation, the act of marriage had shifted from a private matter between two persons into the public domain. The Pharisees asserted the community's right and privilege to decide the validity of marriages.

The Pharisaic edict concerning intermarriage was curious. They did not **prohibit** intermarriage. A prohibition would have forbidden the act, and those involved would have been guilty of violating the law. Instead, they **invalidated** it. They simply decreed it to be a non-act. Instead of creating intermarriage as a crime punishable by law, they ruled it out of existence. A couple who intermarried did not commit a crime, did not violate a law. They simply were not married. Any child born of such a union was illegitimate (a *mamzer*). This Pharisaic/Rabbinic edict is still in force today in the *halacha* (Jewish law) that is binding on all Orthodox and Conservative Jews.

33

Throughout the centuries the Rabbis prevented intermarriage by simply refusing to participate in a ceremony that did not exist. And the Christian clergy also prevented it by refusing to officiate in a wedding ceremony when a Jew was one of the partners. Remember, religious establishments had full control over the institution of marriage until the end of the Eighteenth Century. In the modern period, a century ago, the secular state began to regulate marriage. Couples no longer had to pass muster before the requirements of any religion. In most countries today a couple can be wed without any religious ceremony.*

IN THE UNITED STATES

Information on intermarriage in the United States is somewhat hazy and differs radically from one study to another. The statistics which follow, however, are generally accepted by most scholars. The prime source for the data in this section are several studies reported in various volumes of the *American Jewish Yearbook* (published by the American Jewish Committee and the Jewish Publication Society of America), although some figures have been culled from other sources.

In the early years of this country, 1776-1840, intermarriage rates between Jews and non-Jews was relatively high; 28.7% of all Jews who married during that time married non-Jews. This is not surprising when we consider that the committed Jew, the dedicated and fervently religious Jew, was not the one to set sail for a new land where there were no Jewish communities, no synagogues, no kosher markets, no Jewish teachers, nor any other communal or ritual facilities. With few exceptions, the first Jewish immigrants in America were already somewhat assimilated or

---

*One of the few nations that does not have civil marriage today is the State of Israel. The Rabbinical Court of Israel has ruled (Rabbinical Courts Jurisdiction 1953 Section 2) that intermarriage is illegal. But neither the civil nor ciminal codes of Israel have any punishment for this deed. Thus, Israelis who wish to intermarry—and they exist—must travel outside their country for the ceremony. When they return to Israel, there is no legal way to prevent their marriage from being accepted as valid.

prepared to become so. Even when they came in large groups, hoping to establish Jewish life here, they were prepared to make concessions that contemporary Jews today would find unthinkable. In 1654, the first permanent Jewish settlement was established in New Amsterdam; the Jews who disembarked there were only allowed to do so if they promised not to build a synagogue or create a Jewish cemetery. As these small Jewish communities developed, Jewish merchants traded with non-Jews, shared meals with non-Jews, and many of their children married non-Jews. Actually, the 28.7% figure is amazingly low considering the size and commitment of the earliest Jewish communities in America.

There is no accurate date for the period between 1840 and 1900. In 1900, the collection of intermarriage statistics began in earnest by Jewish scholars and organizations. With the influx of vast numbers of East European Jews into the United States between 1880 and 1920, intermarriage rates dropped significantly. The East European Jews were religiously traditional, culturally non-assimilated, and they developed close-knit communities and communal institutions.

In 1880 there were only 300,000 Jews in the entire United States. Between 1880 and 1920 two million East European Jewish immigrants entered this country. This wave of immigration led to a different sort of "intermarriage." The German Jews who dominated American Jewish life until 1880 created as many barriers as possible to prevent their children from marrying East European Jews whom they saw as the "bearded barbarians," bringing European ghetto life into the United States. A German Jew who came home with an East European Jewish spouse during this period could expect as much of an outburst on the part of his parents as today's Jew bringing home a non-Jew.

The Jewish community gained radically in population; but following the end of mass Jewish immigration into the United States in the 1920's, the incidence of intermarriage began to grow. The majority of American Jews in the beginning of this century were religious, first-generation, East Europeans; their children basically did not marry non-Jews. Since that time, however, continually to the present, the incidence of intermarriage has increased significantly as the Jewish community assimilated into American life.

INTERMARRIAGE RATE

(Percentage of Jews getting married who marry non-Jews)

1900 - 1920	2%
1921 - 1940	3.1%
1941 - 1950	6.7%
1951 - 1960	6.1% (note period of decrease)
1961 - 1965	19.7% to 31.1%
1966 - 1970	48.1%
1971 - 1975	25% to 53.6%

If the 53.6% intermarriage rate is close to reality, and I believe it may well be, only one of every two Jewish children growing up in the United States today will marry a Jew. Remember, if you will, the chart of weddings in the preface. Let's look at that chart again with the idea in mind that intermarriage has exceeded the 50% figure.

Take, for example, four Jewish people who are involved in weddings:

#1 marries a non-Jew.
#2 marries a non-Jew.
#3 marries #4 in a Jewish/Jewish wedding.

THUS, TWO OF EVERY THREE WEDDINGS IN WHICH A JEW PARTICIPATES IS AN INTERMARRIAGE.

Intermarriage has reached epidemic proportions. Ignoring it does no good. Forbidding it does no good. Chastising accomplishes nothing. In every Jewish journal and newspaper, articles abound warning young people of the dangers of intermarriage. From every pulpit rabbis attempt to reinforce sentiment against it. The vast majority of Jewish parents try, from infancy on, to steer their children away from it. This is most vividly seen from the perspective of a campus rabbi whose encounters with parents of new students always center around the possibility of their child meeting other Jewish students. But even in schools where Jewish students are a majority, even in communities which are Jewishly self-contained, young Jews have a way of "breaking out" of the environment and finding non-Jews as marriage partners. The problem is growing more severe. As the rate of intermarriage increases and the number of Jews assimilating away from our community escalates, the very future of the American Jewish community is at stake.

But there is, I believe, a solution. There is a way wherein our grandchildren will be Jewish and the Jewish community will not lose.

Your child is important. You owe it to yourself and to your child to read and consider with an open mind Section III of this book.

II

THE WEDDING CEREMONY

5

A Wedding Is Not A Funeral

A couple planning to enter into an intermarriage usually encounters difficulty trying to arrange for the wedding ceremony. They normally try to get a clergyman from one of their religions to officiate. In all likelihood the religion they choose for the ceremony is dependent upon which set of parents exerts greater pressure.

When they come to me, I ask them why they want a Jewish wedding ceremony. The answer usually goes something like this:

"Well, I'm Jewish. Sue doesn't care which ceremony we use, and I'd like to be able to please my parents."

Deciding the religious nature of the wedding ceremony in order to please the parents is wrong. The couple who "buys" the parents' temporary peace of mind at this price does so at the risk of starting their life together on a note of hypocrisy. It's nice when your child wants to please you, but that should not be the basis of selecting the religious nature of the wedding ceremony.

What, then, should determine it?

The majority of rabbis have a simple guideline to determine whether a Jewish ceremony is appropriate for a couple wishing to wed, and it is this: If both the groom and the bride are Jewish, a

Jewish wedding is appropriate, and if one is not Jewish, a Jewish wedding is not allowed. This is in accordance with *halachic* law.

But what if we have a situation where one of the partners is not Jewish and they (the Jewish partner's parents) want a Jewish wedding ceremony? Of course, it is forbidden by Jewish law.

But there are many rabbis, primarily within the Reform movement, who knowingly and consciously reject this law. It *is* possible to find a rabbi who will officiate, although it may be difficult.

Finding a rabbi should not be the issue. The question ought to be: **SHOULD** THIS INTERMARRYING COUPLE SEEK A RABBI AND A JEWISH WEDDING CEREMONY? In some cases it is appropriate and in others it is not.

The rule of thumb that you might follow in deciding the religious nature of the wedding is this:

A WEDDING IS NOT A FUNERAL

It is amazing how many people confuse a wedding with a funeral. In a Jewish funeral service, the rabbi stands beside the casket and speaks:

"This was a good Jew. He put up with religious school when he was a child; he became *bar mitzvah*. He was active in the synagogue and gave to the U.J.A. and was committed to the Jewish community. Now he is gone, and we are assembled to say 'goodbye' to a Jew who will no longer be with us." Or something like that.

A funeral service is a ritual that is performed at the END of one's life. It is a ritual of termination, a rite of passage **OUTWARD** from the Jewish community.

What, then, of a situation wherein a couple's marrying will effectively end the Jewishness of their home? If a Jew and non-Jew marry, and if that marriage will terminate the practice of Judaism in that family, what kind of ceremony should the rabbi read?—a wedding or a funeral?

Unlike the funeral service which commemorates the passage outward from the Jewish community, the wedding ceremony should be the "keynote" to the marriage itself. It is a ritual of initiation, a rite of passage **INWARD** toward the Jewish community. The wedding ceremony is a ritual that sanctifies the union; the

Jewish wedding ceremony welcomes the new couple into the community.

If Judaism will end for the couple following the wedding ceremony, the couple is obviously not seeking a rite of passage inward, but rather one of termination. The wedding ceremony is not automatically due a Jew for what he used to be. If one seeks a ceremony solely on the grounds of past identity, the appropriate ceremony is the funeral service, not the wedding service.

Thus, in order to determine whether a Jewish wedding ceremony is appropriate, the couple should start from the end and work backward: What will be the religious identity of the couple, of the family, **after** the wedding? If it will be a Jewish family in a Jewish home, then seeking a rabbi for a Jewish wedding can be appropriate. If it will be something else, the couple should forget a Jewish wedding and seek instead a ceremony consistent with its future identity. Only in this way will the ceremony chosen be more than an appeasement to the parents.

Each couple should first determine what their religious identity will be. Will they be a Jewish couple raising Jewish children in a Jewish home and identifying as part of the Jewish community? If so, it is reasonable for them to desire and seek a Jewish wedding.

But if Judaism will end with them—if they do not intend to be a part of the Jewish community and practice Judaism in their home and as a model for their children—a Jewish wedding ceremony is not proper for them. It is not proper regardless of what the parents might want. Supposedly, it causes less "grief" for the Jewish parents if their child is married by a rabbi in a Jewish ceremony, even if that child marries a non-Jew. But is this fair to the child?

Any two people can move in together, set up housekeeping and live as a couple. A couple chooses the ritual of a wedding ceremony as a commitment to each other. They seek a Jewish ceremony in order to sanctify the love they already have. The Hebrew word for wedding ceremony, *Kiddushin,* means "sanctification." And in the Jewish ceremony, the couple will pledge to live Jewish lives, have a Jewish home and raise their children as Jews. This vow is contained in the marriage contract. And during the service itself the couple will vow to live "according to the laws of Moses and Israel." If the bride and groom do not believe what they are promising each other, the beauty of the ceremony will

43

wither. They begin their "sanctified" life together on a sour note of hypocrisy.

The parents have a right not to be embarrassed by the ceremony. But the couple has a greater right to unite their lives in a ceremony that holds sanctity for them.

Which ceremony should they choose?

In the case of intermarrying couples, there are several choices available to them.

(1) Joint Jewish/Christian Ceremony

Assuming that one is Jewish and the other Christian, the couple might decide to try to have a rabbi and a minister (priest) officiate. They think that would resolve the "parental problem" immediately. Both sets of parents will be content that they have not completely "lost." In reality, however, both sets of parents will probably find this compromise less than satisfying.

Also, attempting to find two such clergymen becomes an arduous task. The couple may find a Christian clergyman with comparable ease. But locating a rabbi who will participate with a Christian minister in a wedding ceremony is virtually impossible. Most rabbis will not do it; nor will they even refer the couple to the few rabbis who will.

Why?

A joint Jewish/Christian ceremony is neither Jewish nor Christian. It is inauthentic to both religious traditions. To request this of a rabbi is *chutzpah*. To expect the rabbi to say "Yes" is not realistic. The state has given the rabbi the right to officiate at weddings **only because he represents the tradition of the Jewish people.** The rabbi is not a secular officer of the state; he represents the Jewish tradition. To expect him to officiate in a joint (i.e. non-Jewish) ceremony is asking him to violate the mandate that allows him to marry couples in the first place.

I never cease to be amazed when I explain that I cannot be a part of a joint wedding ceremony. The couple—and the parents—usually get angry with me. They charge me with forgetting "the brotherhood of man." But would that same couple go to an attorney and ask him to violate his professional standards by perjuring himself or falsifying testimony? Surely not.

Unless the couple happens to find one of the few rabbis who

44

will participate in this kind of ceremony, the couple should expect to be turned down when making this request.

(2) A Christian Ceremony

The couple will have much better luck should they decide to have a Christian clergyman officiate in a Christian wedding ceremony. (Some Christian clergy, notably those of the establishment "high church" denominations, still have difficulty condoning a Christian ceremony if both partners are not Christian. But many of the clergy of the denominations with no fixed liturgy find little difficulty in accomodating the couple).

As a campus rabbi for several years, I found myself working with non-Jewish as well as Jewish students. Non-Jewish students would come to me for counseling or for classes. One couple asked me to perform their wedding ceremony, although neither was Jewish. I was admittedly flattered, but I felt I had to decline. While speaking with them further, however, I discovered that they were not Christian either. In an effort to be helpful, I called a colleague, a Protestant chaplain on the campus, and asked if he would officiate. "Yes," he said. "I will be happy to officiate. I've never refused to marry any couple. I just don't know where I would set limits." Judaism, however, has limits, limits imposed by standards and laws and tradition.

So a Christian ceremony is frequently possible.

(3) A Jewish Ceremony

A couple comes to a rabbi. One partner is Jewish and one is not. Neither is planning to convert to the religion of the other. But they have decided that they want a Jewish wedding ceremony. What is the rabbi's response?

If the rabbi is Orthodox or Conservative or Reconstructionist, he will not—can not—officiate. The law is clear: both partners must be Jewish.

If they go to a Reform rabbi, the variety of responses would fill a volume. Most Reform rabbis, some 60%, will not officiate at an intermarriage. But 40% of the Reform rabbinate will—under certain circumstances. And those circumstances vary from rabbi to rabbi.

—Some will officiate if the non-Jew plans to convert later.

—Some will officiate if the couple promises to have a Jewish home and raise their children as Jews.

—Some will officiate if the couple will join the temple.

—Some will officiate simply if no Christian ceremony will be part of the ritual.

—Some will officiate if the non-Jew first takes a course of study in Judaism.

—Some will officiate if the Jewish partner's parents are already members of his congregation.

The list is endless.

How does a Reform rabbi determine what standards he will keep? It is a matter of his own conscience. The central body of Reform rabbis (Central Conference of American Rabbis) calls upon Reform rabbis to discourage intermarriage but does not prohibit their officiating at them. Some of the justifications that these forty-percent of the Reform rabbinate offer for their participating in intermarriage ceremonies are:

"By turning the couple away, we have lost another family for the Jewish people. By bringing Jewish rituals into their lives at such an important time, we still have a chance to retain them."

"The non-Jew is not at present prepared to convert. But the couple plans in every other way to identify Jewishly."

"The wedding is scheduled so soon that the only way the non-Jew could convert would be through a 'quickie' conversion. And I would rather officiate at an intermarriage than make a sham of the conversion process."

"By giving the couple a Jewish wedding, we have a better chance of retaining their children. A 1970 study showed that 87.8% of intermarried couples who were married by a rabbi were giving their children a Jewish education. And that is quite impressive when one considers that the national average for Jewish couples is only 80%!"

If you are looking for a rabbi to officiate at an intermarriage, finding him is a joy. But rest assured that many Jews look with disdain at such practices.

(4) A Secular Ceremony

If the couple cannot fully agree on the religion of their home, if their religious identity will be neither fully Jewish nor Christian, then either of these religious ceremonies is inappropriate.

There is nothing wrong with a couple being married in a secular ceremony by a justice of the peace. Sure, it lacks the rituals we might expect. But what value are meaningless rituals? A secular wedding can be done nicely, as ornately as the bride and groom desire. For many intermarrying couples, this is the best solution.

(5) Conversion

The most logical solution to an impending intermarriage is for one of the partners to convert and thus remove a majority of the problems they face. If they really cannot agree on a unified religion in their home, they probably are not ready for marriage—at least not to each other. But if they are determined to make a go of it, if they have the will and the fortitude to create a life together that will last and be meaningful, they ought to seriously consider the possibility of one of them converting to the other's religion.

The partner with the weaker tie to his religion and heritage should make an attempt to adopt the other's religion. He might find, given a chance, a sense of fulfillment in the new religion. And once converted, it is no longer an intermarriage. The couple's chances at making their marriage succeed increases. It brings them closer together. They are able to create a unified home.

The last section of this volume will go into the issue of conversion in detail.

JOINING THE COMMUNITY

Regardless of the wedding ceremony the couple chooses, the ramifications after the wedding can be harsh. If there is no conversion, and the couple wishes to affiliate with a Jewish congregation, there may be difficulty.

REFORM congregations generally accept intermarried couples into the membership of their congregations. Their children will be granted the right of religious education, regardless of which partner is Jewish.

CONSERVATIVE congregations, until some years ago, refused membership to intermarried couples. But since 1963, the Jewish spouse of an intermarriage can join a Conservative congregation. If the Jewish spouse is the wife, the children are also Jewish (according to Jewish law) and are entitled to a religious education. But if the Jewish spouse is the husband, the children (non-Jewish, according to Jewish law) will be denied a religious education.

RECONSTRUCTIONIST congregations, while prohibiting rabbis from officiating at intermarriages, regard the intermarried Jew as still being a Jew, although one who has disobeyed a religious mandate. Many Reconstructionist congregations will accept the family into the congregation after the intermarriage has taken place.

ORTHODOX congregations will neither accept for membership nor provide education for intermarried couples and their children.

6

The Jewish Wedding Ceremony

Some rabbis will officiate at a Jewish wedding ceremony only using the "approved" version of the text according to their affiliation. Most rabbis, however, are more than willing to read any addition the bride and groom would like in their wedding. This can be done without harming the religious nature of the ceremony. In many cases additional material can enhance it.

Most of the additions to the wedding ceremony that I have seen have been in good taste and have had special meaning for the couple.

One couple wrote love poems to each other that they read immediately following their vow.

Another couple, in an outdoor wedding, left the *chuppa* to plant a tree in their yard. They had researched the meaning of trees in Judaism. It was a symbolic expression of the love they felt for each other.

There are, of course, other kinds of "additions" that don't follow the pattern . . .

One young couple came to me some years ago when I was Hillel director at Northwestern University in Evanston, Illinois. It was late summer, but they appeared to be sweating far more than the weather would warrant. They were nervous. I remember the groom telling me that they wanted to be married the following summer. Then he timidly stated, "We'd like to get married on June 20th—at sunrise."

"Hmmm," I thought. "Very unique." As nonchalantly as possible, I opened my calendar, thumbed through it, looked up and said, "Very well. It seems I don't have any other appointments for sunrise on June 20th."

Still, the couple was not relieved. There was more. Finally it came out. "Well, you see," the groom stuttered, "we'd like to be married **in** Lake Michigan. We met while we were swimming there."

I had instant visions of the bride dressed in a white bathing suit, the groom in a black bathing suit and bow tie, *kippot* floating off the heads of the wedding party as the waves lapped over them, the rabbi bobbing up and down, trying to read the ceremony while keeping the *Ketubah* dry.

Although it was a bit unusual, I agreed to officiate at this wedding. (I could only sigh in relief that they weren't sky divers.)

Most couples who come to a rabbi for a wedding really do not know what to expect. They do not know whether they will be allowed to personalize their wedding with additional readings or an unusual style. It probably would be helpful to the couple if they had some knowledge and understanding of the basic wedding ceremony before seeking to add to it or change it.

This is the Jewish wedding ceremony:

1. The Signing of the *Ketubah*.

Prior to the wedding ceremony, the bride and groom sign the ketubah, *or marriage contract, in the presence of two witnesses. Originally the* Ketubah *was used as the primary legal document transferring property (the bride) from her father to her husband. Most modern* Ketubot, *however, have removed the sexist origins of the document and instead serve as contractual agreements between the two partners.*

2. The Wedding Party Assembles under the *Chuppa*.

The processional varies from wedding to wedding at the option of the couple. How the wedding party enters is a matter of social custom,

not religious dictate. The processional ends with the wedding party un-
der and around the chuppa. *The rabbi faces the couple; the bride's at-*
tendant (maid or matron of honor) is at her side; the groom's attendant
(best man) is at his side. In some weddings the parents of the couple
also stand at the chuppa.

3. Introductory Prayers*

Rabbi:

Blessed be he that cometh in the
name of the Lord.

בָּרוּךְ הַבָּא בְּשֵׁם יְיָ.
בֵּרַכְנוּכֶם מִבֵּית יְיָ:

Serve the Lord with gladness; come
before Him with singing.

O God, supremely blessed, supreme.
in might and glory, guide and bless
this bridegroom and bride.

עִבְדוּ אֶת־יְיָ בְּשִׂמְחָה.
בֹּאוּ לְפָנָיו בִּרְנָנָה:

מִי אַדִּיר עַל הַכֹּל. מִי
בָּרוּךְ עַל הַכֹּל. מִי גָדוֹל
עַל הַכֹּל. יְבָרֵךְ אֶת־הֶחָתָן
וְאֶת־הַכַּלָּה:

Unto Thee, O God and Father, we lift our souls in praise. All creation declares Thy glory; through man, fashioned in Thine image,
Thou hast revealed Thy majesty. Within his heart Thou hast
implanted the ennobling influences of love and devotion. Thou Who
art the Source of life and of joy, bless the covenant which this
bridegroom and bride now seal in Thy name. Be with them in this
sacred hour and in all the days to come. Amen.

4. Perambulation

In the Orthodox wedding ceremony the bride walks around the
groom four or seven times, depending upon local custom. This is not
customary in other Jewish wedding ceremonies.

---

*Quotations in this chapter are reprinted from *Rabbi's Manual.* © Central
Conference of American Rabbis. 1961, and used with its permission.

5. Betrothal Kiddush

In antiquity there were two wedding ceremonies. First, the bride and groom entered the formal bethrothal or engagement status with a ceremony. In this ceremony a kiddush over wine was recited; in it was a reminder that the couple are forbidden sexual contact until the final wedding ceremony. In later years, the betrothal and the marriage (kiddushin) *ceremonies were combined into one ceremony.*

In the **Orthodox** *ceremony, the betrothal kiddush is recited at this point in the ceremony. The groom and bride then drink from the cup.*

In the **Conservative** *ceremony the betrothal kiddush is also a part of the ritual. However, in the Conservative wedding the original Hebrew is sung but it is never translated into English.*

The **Reform** *ceremony omits this ritual, since by the end of the wedding the couple will be fully married. Thus, the reminder to abstain from sexual relations is no longer necessary.*

6. Acceptance

Rabbi: Do you (name of groom) take (name of bride) to be your wife, promising to cherish and protect her, whether in good fortune or in adversity, and to seek together with her a life hallowed by the faith of Israel?

Groom responds in the affiirmative.

Rabbi: Do you (name of bride) take (name of Groom) to be your husband, promising to cherish and protect him, whether in good fortune or in adversity, and to seek together with him a life hallowed by the faith of Israel?

Bride responds in the affirmative.

The Conservative ceremony omits the Acceptance as part of the ceremony, feeling that it has already taken place prior to the wedding when the couple signed the ketubah.

7. The Vow

In Reform ceremonies the reading of the Seven Benedictions usually precedes the vow.

Rabbi: As you (name of groom) place this ring upon the finger of your bride, speak to her these words:

The best man hands the groom the ring. The groom places it on the finger of the bride (traditionally the forefinger of the right hand) and recites the vow after the rabbi:

52

הֲרֵי אַתְּ מְקֻדֶּשֶׁת לִי בְּטַבַּעַת זוֹ כְּדָת מֹשֶׁה וְיִשְׂרָאֵל:

With this ring be thou consecrated unto me as my wife according to the law of God and the faith of Israel.

Rabbi: And you (name of bride) *(If double ring ceremony, add:* place this ring upon your bridegroom's finger as a token of wedlock and) say unto him these words:

If it is a double ring ceremony, the maid/matron of honor hands the bride the groom's ring. The bride places the ring on the finger of the groom and recites the vow after the rabbi. If it is a single ring ceremony, the bride recites the vow without the additional phrase.

הֲרֵי אַתָּה מְקֻדָּשׁ לִי (בְּטַבַּעַת זוֹ) כְּדָת מֹשֶׁה וְיִשְׂרָאֵל:

(With this ring) be thou consecrated unto me as my husband according to the law of God and the faith of Israel.

This is the central part of the wedding ceremony.

If a couple wishes to add some creative element to their wedding, this is an appropriate time.

8. The Reading of the *Ketubah*

The rabbi reads the ketubah *(marriage contract) that has been signed by the groom and bride and witnessed. In some Reform ceremonies there is no* ketubah.

9. The Seven Benedictions

(1) Traditional benedictions:

53

בָּרוּךְ אַתָּה יְיָ אֱלֹהֵינוּ מֶלֶךְ הָעוֹלָם בּוֹרֵא פְּרִי הַגָּפֶן:

בָּרוּךְ אַתָּה יְיָ אֱלֹהֵינוּ מֶלֶךְ הָעוֹלָם שֶׁהַכֹּל בָּרָא
לִכְבוֹדוֹ:

בָּרוּךְ אַתָּה יְיָ אֱלֹהֵינוּ מֶלֶךְ הָעוֹלָם יוֹצֵר הָאָדָם:

בָּרוּךְ אַתָּה יְיָ אֱלֹהֵינוּ מֶלֶךְ הָעוֹלָם אֲשֶׁר יָצַר אֶת־
הָאָדָם בְּצַלְמוֹ. בְּצֶלֶם דְּמוּת תַּבְנִיתוֹ. וְהִתְקִין לוֹ מִמֶּנּוּ
בִּנְיַן עֲדֵי עַד. בָּרוּךְ אַתָּה יְיָ יוֹצֵר הָאָדָם:

שׂוֹשׂ תָּשִׂישׂ וְתָגֵל הָעֲקָרָה. בְּקִבּוּץ בָּנֶיהָ לְתוֹכָהּ בְּשִׂמְחָה.
בָּרוּךְ אַתָּה יְיָ מְשַׂמֵּחַ צִיּוֹן בְּבָנֶיהָ:

שַׂמֵּחַ תְּשַׂמַּח רֵעִים הָאֲהוּבִים. כְּשַׂמֵּחֲךָ יְצִירְךָ בְּגַן עֵדֶן
מִקֶּדֶם. בָּרוּךְ אַתָּה יְיָ מְשַׂמֵּחַ חָתָן וְכַלָּה:

בָּרוּךְ אַתָּה יְיָ אֱלֹהֵינוּ מֶלֶךְ הָעוֹלָם אֲשֶׁר בָּרָא שָׂשׂוֹן
וְשִׂמְחָה. חָתָן וְכַלָּה. גִּילָה רִנָּה. דִּיצָה וְחֶדְוָה. אַהֲבָה וְאַחֲוָה.
שָׁלוֹם וְרֵעוּת. מְהֵרָה יְיָ אֱלֹהֵינוּ יִשָּׁמַע בְּעָרֵי יְהוּדָה
וּבְחוּצוֹת יְרוּשָׁלָיִם. קוֹל שָׂשׂוֹן וְקוֹל שִׂמְחָה. קוֹל חָתָן וְקוֹל
כַּלָּה. קוֹל מִצְהֲלוֹת חֲתָנִים מֵחֻפָּתָם וּנְעָרִים מִמִּשְׁתֵּה נְגִינָתָם.
בָּרוּךְ אַתָּה יְיָ מְשַׂמֵּחַ חָתָן עִם־הַכַּלָּה:

Blessed art Thou, O Lord our God, Ruler of the universe, Creator of the fruit of the vine.

Blessed art Thou, O Lord our God, Ruler of the universe, Who created everything for Thy glory.

Blessed art Thou, O Lord our God, Ruler of the universe, Creator of man.

Blessed art Thou, O Lord our God, Who created man in Thine image and in Thy likeness. Blessed art Thou, O Lord, Who hast created man.

May the childless Zion be extremely glad and rejoice with her in joy. Blessed art Thou, O Lord, Who causest Zion to be glad at her children's return.

May Thou gladden this couple as Thou gladdened the first couple in the Garden of Eden. Blessed art Thou, O Lord our God, Who bringest joy to the groom and the bride.

Blessed art Thou, O Lord our God, Ruler of the universe, Who created joy and gladness, groom and bride, rejoicing, song, happiness and delight, love and harmony, peace and companionship. May there soon be heard in the cities of Judah and in the streets of Jerusalem voices of joy and gladness, voices of groom and bride, the jubilent voices of grooms from the *chupa,* and young people feasting and singing.

(2) **Shortened Form of Seven Benedictions:**

בָּרוּךְ אַתָּה יְיָ אֱלֹהֵינוּ מֶלֶךְ הָעוֹלָם שֶׁהַכֹּל בָּרָא
לִכְבוֹדוֹ:

בָּרוּךְ אַתָּה יְיָ אֱלֹהֵינוּ מֶלֶךְ הָעוֹלָם יוֹצֵר הָאָדָם:

בָּרוּךְ אַתָּה יְיָ אֱלֹהֵינוּ מֶלֶךְ הָעוֹלָם אֲשֶׁר יָצַר אֶת־
הָאָדָם בְּצַלְמוֹ. בְּצֶלֶם דְּמוּת תַּבְנִיתוֹ. וְהִתְקִין לוֹ מִמֶּנּוּ
בִּנְיַן עֲדֵי עַד. בָּרוּךְ אַתָּה יְיָ יוֹצֵר הָאָדָם:

בָּרוּךְ אַתָּה יְיָ אֱלֹהֵינוּ מֶלֶךְ הָעוֹלָם אֲשֶׁר בָּרָא שָׂשׂוֹן
וְשִׂמְחָה. חָתָן וְכַלָּה. גִּילָה רִנָּה. דִּיצָה וְחֶדְוָה. אַהֲבָה
וְאַחֲוָה. שָׁלוֹם וְרֵעוּת. שַׂמַּח תְּשַׂמַּח רֵעִים הָאֲהוּבִים. וְיִזְכּוּ
לִבְנוֹת בַּיִת בְּיִשְׂרָאֵל לְשֵׁם וְלִתְהִלָּה. וִיהִי שָׁלוֹם בְּבֵיתָם
וְשַׁלְוָה וְהַשְׁקֵט בְּלִבּוֹתָם. וְיִרְאוּ בְנֶחָמַת יִשְׂרָאֵל וּבִתְשׁוּעַת
עוֹלָם. בָּרוּךְ אַתָּה יְיָ מְשַׂמֵּחַ חָתָן עִם־הַכַּלָּה:

בָּרוּךְ אַתָּה יְיָ אֱלֹהֵינוּ מֶלֶךְ הָעוֹלָם בּוֹרֵא פְּרִי הַגָּפֶן:

Blessed art Thou, O Lord our God, Ruler of the Universe, Who hast created all things for Thy glory.

Blessed art Thou, O Lord our God, Ruler of the Universe, Creator of man.

Blessed art Thou, O Lord our God, Ruler of the Universe, Who hast fashioned us in Thine own image and hast established marriage for the fulfillment and perpetuation of life in accordance with Thy holy purpose. Blessed art Thou, O Lord, Creator of man.

Blessed art Thou, O Lord our God, Ruler of the Universe, Who art the source of all gladness and joy. Through Thy grace we attain affection, companionship and peace. Grant, O Lord, that the love which unites this bridegroom and bride may grow in abiding happiness. May their family life be ennobled through their devotion to the faith of Israel. May there be peace in their home, quietness and confidence in their hearts. May they be sustained by Thy comforting presence in the midst of our people and by Thy promise of salvation for all mankind. Blessed art Thou, O Lord, Who dost unite bridegroom and bride in holy joy.

Blessed art Thou, O Lord our God, Ruler of the Universe, Creator of the fruit of the vine.

(3) Alternative English translation by Everett Gendler*

You abound in blessings, Lord our God, Source of all creation, Creator of the fruit of the vine.

You abound in blessings, Lord our God, Source of all creation, all of whose creations reflect Your glory.

You abound in blessings, Lord our God, Source of all creation, Creator of human beings.

You abound in blessings, Lord our God, Source of all creation, who created man and woman in Your image so that they might live, love, and so perpetuate life. You abound in blessings, Lord, Creator of human beings.

We all rejoice as these two persons, overcoming separateness, unite in joy. You abound in blessings, Lord, permitting us to share in others' joy.

May these lovers rejoice as did the first man and woman in the primordial Garden of Eden. You abound in blessings, Lord, Source of joy for bride and groom.

10. The *Kiddush*

Since the kiddush *was recited in the Seven Benedictions, the rabbi now hands the wine cup to the groom who drinks from it and then passes it to the bride who drinks from it.*

Rabbi: As you have shared the wine from this cup, so may you, with God's guidance, draw contentment, comfort and felicity from the cup of life. May you find all life's joys heightened, its bitterness sweetened, and all things hallowed by true companionship and love.

The Conservative ceremony adds a reading from the Song of Songs at this point in the ceremony.

---

*From THE FIRST JEWISH CATALOGUE by Michael Strassfeld, Sharon Strassfeld & Richard Siegel. © 1973. The Jewish Publication Society of America. Reprinted with permission.

11. Pronouncement

Rabbi: בָּרוּךְ אַתָּה יְיָ מְקַדֵּשׁ עַמּוֹ יִשְׂרָאֵל עַל יְדֵי (חֻפָּה וְ) קִדּוּשִׁין:

Blessed art Thou, O God, who sanctifiest Thy people Israel by the covenant of the marriage.

In the presence of this company as witness you have spoken the words and performed the rites which unite your lives. I, therefore, declare you (name of groom) and you (name of bride) husband and wife, married in accordance with the laws of the State of (name) and according to the tradition of our Jewish faith.

And now I ask you and all your dear ones to bow your heads in reverence. Silently let us pray that God will bless your home and help you to achieve your highest hopes.

12. Conclusion

The rabbi places his hands on the couple.

Rabbi:

יְבָרֶכְךָ יְיָ וְיִשְׁמְרֶךָ:

יָאֵר יְיָ פָּנָיו אֵלֶיךָ וִיחֻנֶּךָּ:

יִשָּׂא יְיָ פָּנָיו אֵלֶיךָ וְיָשֵׂם לְךָ שָׁלוֹם:

May the Lord bless thee and keep thee.

May the Lord cause His countenance to shine upon thee and be gracious unto thee.

May the Lord lift up His countenance unto thee and give thee peace. Amen.

The groom steps on the glass. (The breaking of the glass at the end of the wedding ceremony is one of the oldest rituals in Judaism. Its meaning has undergone many changes through the ages, and countless are the reasons offered for continuing the practice today. The simplest explanation for non-traditional Jews is that it is a revered custom, and without it, there is a feeling that the wedding ceremony has not properly ended.)

The couple kiss.

13. Conclusion

The wedding party leave the chupa, *normally in the reverse order that they entered, with the bride and groom departing first.*

III

THE CASE FOR CONVERSION

7

Conversion and the Jewish Tradition

This chapter is an unabashed sales pitch. No gimmicks, no euphamisms, no pretense. They really aren't needed. You are reading this book presumably because you or someone close to you is facing an intermarriage.

You may feel desperate. You certainly are concerned. What can be done? The parental response to intermarriage is rarely approval. More often than not, the Jewish parents anguish over the reality and lash out at their child in hostility and grief.

Most parents sincerely believe that they can exert some control over their child's decision to marry a non-Jew. But this simply is not true. At the point when the child has decided to intermarry, any action on the part of the parents to stop the impending marriage is futile.

The solution offered here is based on the view that the marriage plans cannot be changed.

THERE IS NO POSSIBLE ACTION ON THE PART
OF THE PARENT WHICH IS GOING TO CAUSE

THE CHILD TO REJECT THE CHOSEN NON-
JEWISH MATE.

As the Rabbis would say, "There are two possibilities . . ."—
and so there are in this as well. One possibility is that the parent's
response toward the couple will turn the Jewish child away from
Judaism; rejection and hostility will insure this result. The second
possibility, however, is that the parent can bring the non-Jew into
the fold of the Jewish people.

In my experience of counseling hundreds of conversion students, I have found that the greatest obstacle the convert must
face is rejection from the Jewish parents of the intended spouse.
They so often heap abuse, anger and hostility upon one who
wishes to become Jewish!

Not only does this parental behavior become counter-
productive; it is diametrically opposed to Jewish tradition.

THE THREE RABBIS

There is an old saw which says that if a prospective convert
approaches an Orthodox rabbi, the rabbi will immediately kick
him out. If he approaches the rabbi a second time, the rabbi will
sit him down and tell him all the reasons why he should not convert to Judaism, and then kick him out again. If he should approach the same rabbi a third time, the rabbi will accept him as a
student.

If the prospective conversion student should approach a
Conservative rabbi, the rabbi will sit him down and tell him why
he should not convert; then he will kick him out. If he approaches
the rabbi a second time, the rabbi will accept him as a student.

If, however, the prospective convert approaches a Reform
rabbi, the rabbi will give him books and inform him of the date of
the next conversion class.

Obviously this story is based on stereotypes which do not
translate into real life. The assumption of most people is that the
Orthodox rabbi is upholding the tradition while the Reform rabbi
is violating it. But is this accurate? What does the tradition say
about conversion to Judaism?

THE BIBLICAL PERIOD

The first Jew, Abraham, is considered by tradition to have been a convert. Reference is made to him as "a wandering Aramean" in Deuteronomy (26:5).

The technical term for convert is *ger*. Rabbinic tradition differentiates between *ger toshav* (resident alien) and *ger tzadik* (righteous convert). In the biblical period there was no formal structure for conversion. The resident alien simply came under the protection and communal structure of the Jewish people.

As you are, so shall be the *ger* before God.
—Numbers 15:15

The *ger* who dewells with you shall be to you as the homeborn and you shall love him as yourself.
—Leviticus 19:34

As the biblical period progressed, it became more common to accept converts to Judaism. At one point it became common practice to actually go out to seek them. Today's Jewish community shudders at the thought of proselytism (missionary activity)—but look at the words of Isaiah:

God will have pity upon Jacob and once more take Israel as His own, resettling them in their own country where converts shall join them and attach themselves to the household of Jacob.
—Isaiah 14:1

Here is the message of God . . . be a light unto the nations, to open eyes that are blind . . .
—Isaiah 42:4 ff

The rules of my religion I send forth to enlighten every nation.
—Isaiah 51:4

Isaiah was not alone. The prophet Jeremiah said:

In those days they will call Jerusalem "the throne of God" and all nations shall gather to it living no longer by superstitions of their benighted minds.
—Jeremiah 3:17

Or the words of Ezekiel:

You must allot (this land) among yourselves and among the converts who bring up families among you. They are to count as natives . . .
—Ezekiel 47:21 ff.

Perhaps the most stirring of all statements comes from the Prophet Zechariah:

"In those days," the Lord of Hosts declares, "ten men from nations of every language will seize the robe of a single Jew and say, 'We will go with you, for we have heard that God is with you.' "
Zechariah 8:22-23

Throughout all of biblical literature there are many references to conversion to Judaism. Almost all treat it positively and matter-of-factly.

The only negative voices against conversion to Judaism in the entire Bible are Ezra and Nehemiah, who from an historical perspective, were faced with the overwhelming burden of trying to create a viable, unified people from the remnant that returned from the Babylonian Exile. In fact some scholars feel that the Book of Ruth, which is read every *Shavuot* holiday, was written as a rejoinder to Ezra and Nehemiah. Ruth, a Moabite woman who married a Jew, converted to Judaism only **after** the death of her husband. Her vow to Naomi, her Jewish mother-in-law, is considered by many as the most poetic of all biblical verses (Ruth 1:16; see page 31).

THE RABBINIC PERIOD

Following the Exile in the year 70 C.E., significant changes overcame the Jewish people. Uprooted from their homeland, their numbers diminished and dispersed, a "fence around the Torah"— a freezing of interpretation, a protective "wall" around the Law— was established to sustain the people and their faith. One of the results of this "fence" was a reversal from the previous missionary zeal of the Jewish people. From that time on there were no mass conversions to Judaism as there previously had been. Seeking converts ended, yes; but the accepting attitude toward those who voluntarily entered Judaism on their own did not change.

In fact, the Exile of 70 C.E. was felt to have been caused by God so that Jews would scatter among the peoples of the world, influence them, that they would also become Jews. This concept is found in the Talmud *(Pesachim* 87B) as well as in the apocryphal work of Tobit:

> Extol God before the gentiles, ye children of Israel, because for this purpose has He scattered us among them.
>
> —Tobit 13:3

In those days converts to Judaism were highly revered by the Rabbis. The Rabbis, in order to praise biblical characters, described them as converts to Judaism:

(1) Abraham, in the story we all learned in religious school, broke his father's idols, becoming Judaism's first convert. He is cited as the first convert in *Sukkot* 49B.

(2) Isaac was considered a missionary. *(Genesis Raba* 84:4)

(3) Judah's wife, Tamar, is considered to have been a convert. *(Sotah* 10A)

(4) Jacob's daughter, Dinah, is said to have converted Job. *(Genesis Raba* 76)

(5) Moses' father-in-law, Jethro, in one Midrash is depicted as a convert who plans to return to his people and convert them to Judaism. *(Tanhuma* B6)

(6) The Prophet Obidiah is spoken of by Rabbi Meir as a convert. *(Sanhedrin* 39B)

(7) Maimonides considered the exalted Rabbi Akiba to have been the son of a convert. (Introduction to *Mishneh Torah)*

This is but a small sampling of the extensive citations of this nature. They run throughout all strata of Rabbinic literature: the period of the *Tannaim* (to the end of the Second Century C.E.), the *Amoraim* (Third through Fifth Centuries), and the *Savoraim* (Sixth Century)—the periods of time during which the *Talmud* was written. The Rabbis not only interpreted biblical heroes as converts to Judaism, they also spoke positively of contemporary converts. One *Midrash* tells us that a convert who studies Torah is as meritorious as the High Priest.

The *Talmud* even had a standard test for conversion. According to the *Talmud (Yebamot* 47) "If a man comes and says, 'I wish to be a Jew but I am unworthy,' convert him immediately!" The test, you see, was sincerity.

Perhaps the best known Rabbinic story of conversion involved the sage, Hillel. A non-Jew came to Hillel, not really wanting to convert but to taunt the great teacher. He told Hillel that he would convert to Judaism if Hillel could teach him all there is to know about Judaism while standing on one foot. Hillel paused a moment, then said, "What is hateful to you, do not unto your neighbor. All the rest is commentary. Now, go and study!" *(Shabbat* 31A) The scoffer was so moved by the simple profundity of Hillel's words that he began studying and later converted.

You want more than Rabbinic stories? Well, what about historical facts?

The Greek writer of the First Century, Strabo, referred to Jewish missionaries, albeit as a nuisance and problem for the Greeks.

Josephus, the great historian of the Roman era, mentioned by name many of the Roman converts to Judaism. One, Flavius Clemens, was in line for the Imperial throne; but following his conversion, the Emperor had him executed. The wife of Nero worshipped regularly in a synagogue.

Dio Cassius, a Third Century Roman historian, writing about the First Century, stated that ". . . Jews had flocked to Rome in great numbers and were converting many of the natives to their ways . . ."* And to the list of chroniclers of mass Jewish efforts at conversion we can add the names of Seneca, Tacitus, Horace and Juvenal.

In the Fifth Century we find examples of entire villages converting to Judaism. The Rabbis commented on this in the *Talmud (Avoda Zara* 64A). Some notable churchmen publicly became

---

*Heinrich Graetz. *Die judischen Proselyten im Romerreiche unter den Kaisern Domitian, Nerva, Trajan und Hadrian.* Breslau. 1884. Cited in Bernard J. Bamberger. *Proselytism in the Talmudic Period.* Ktav Publishing House. New York. 1939.

Jews, such as Bishop Alemann Bodo (Ninth Century) and Father Wecelinus, Court Chaplain of the German Empire (Eleventh Century).

Perhaps the best known conversion to Judaism was the Kingdom of Khazaria. In the Eighth Century the royal family converted to Judaism and the people soon followed their example. For almost two hundred years the powerful monarchy of Khazaria, to which all surrounding nations paid tribute, was a Jewish kingdom in Eastern Europe.

Less well known than the Khazars, but just as significant, was the Jewish Kingdom of Yemen. In the middle of the Fourth Century the King of Yemen converted to Judaism, and all his subjects followed him into his new religion. For almost two hundred years this kingdom in the Arabian peninsula was a Jewish land. Not only were they all Jews, but they (Hold your breath!) believed in missionary work by the power of the sword. They converted many of their neighbors to Judaism by force. But, in 525 C.E., Dhu Nowas, King of Yemen, invaded Ethiopia in order to convert the Etheopian Christians to Judaism. He was defeated in battle, and the victorious Christians forced an end to Judaism in Yemen.

A remnant of this missionary fervor can even be found in the High Holy Day prayerbook. In the traditional *Rosh Hashana Musaf* service, right in the middle of the *Amidah,* we find the prayer:

All the world shall come to serve You,
    And bless Your glorious name,
And Your righteousness triumphant
    The islands shall acclaim.
And the peoples shall go seeking,
    Who knew You not before,
And the ends of earth shall praise You,
    And tell Your greatness o'er.

They shall build for You their alters,
    Their idols overthrown,
And their graven gods shall shame them,
    As they turn to You alone.
They shall worship You at sunrise,
    And feel Your Kingdom's might,
And impart their understanding,
    To those astray in night.

69

They shall testify Your greatness,
   And of Your power speak,
And extol You, shrined, uplifted,
   Beyond man's highest peak.
And with reverential homage,
   Of love and wonder born,
With the ruler's crown of beauty,
   Your head they shall adorn.

With the coming of Your Kingdom,
   The hills will shout with song,
And the islands laugh exultant,
   That they to God belong.
And all their congregations,
   So loud Your praise shall sing,
That the uttermost peoples, hearing,
   Shall hail You crowned King.

THE MODERN PERIOD

In the Sixteenth Century, Jews of Hungary readily accepted as converts large numbers of Christians who sought out Judaism in order to escape the anti-Christian harrassment of Suleiman and Magnificent. During this time, also, the Jews of Transylvania openly sought converts to Judaism.

Conversion to Judaism was such a normal part of the Jewish routine in the Middle Ages that the *Shulchan Auruch* (Sixteenth Century) dealt with the subject of conversion as a matter of routine. And in the Eighteenth Century, Elijah of Vilna, the Vilna *Gaon,* wrote that "the poor Jew and the convert are as precious to God as any other Jew." (Commentary to Leviticus 19:10)

With all these positive statements and actions concerning conversion, it seems surprising that in the modern Jewish world there are some who discourage conversion to Judaism. Regardless of what they call themselves, those who discourage conversion to Judaism are in opposition to Jewish tradition. When these people are asked for some traditional support against accepting converts, they usually quote Rabbi Chelbo. In *Kiddushin* 70B he stated: "Converts are as hard on Israel as a skin sore." (Some translate: "leprosy.") This statement was felt to be so contrary to the general thrust of Rabbinic literature that the commentators were called upon to explain Rabbi Chelbo's words. *Tosafot* interpreted it as:

"Converts are as hard on Israel as a skin sore because converts are more observant, and they expose the laxity of other Jews."

Another argument one often hears in opposition to conversion is that the convert must want to convert for the sake of Judaism, not for marriage. The majority who are seeking to join the Jewish people today, however, are contemplating marriage to a Jew. But this alone does not give the entire picture.

The **initial** reason for conversion should not matter. What motivates a person to seek conversion to Judaism is not important. The only criterion should be the sincerity of the convert *immediately prior to* conversion. In all likelihood, with proper rabbinic guidance, a prospective convert who enters into study primarily for marriage will ultimately desire Judaism for itself. Once exposed to the richness of our heritage, few conversion students can turn their backs on it. Almost all of the conversion students whom I accept are originally motivated by marriage. But not a single one converts for that reason. In every case, they either undergo an internal transformation or drop out of the program.

Wild boast? Far from it. During the thirteen years that I have been training converts, seven of those students who had begun the process in order to wed a Jew decided to break off the engagement. Had marriage to a Jew been the prime motivation for conversion, that would have been the time, with the wedding plans disintegrated, for the prospective convert to withdraw. In every one of these seven cases, the conversion student continued to study—and became a Jew! In every one of these situations the conversion student had already crossed over that mysterious bridge from non-Jew to Jew—had internalized his Jewish identity—and was unable to reject the new identification he had chosen.

A CROSSOVER

One case, which happened only recently, was especially striking. The couple was geographically separated, and the non-Jew, without telling the Jewish mate-to-be, began a conversion program.

A few months later, when they had a chance to be together, the conversion student discovered that the Jew, too, was doing the same thing. The Jew had become a Christian. The partner who was originally Christian might have been expected to rejoice at this discovery. Instead, she was aghast and informed him that she could not

71

give up her new-found Jewish identity; nor was she (the conversion student) prepared to marry a Christian.

So, where does the anti-conversion sentiment in the Jewish community come from?

ORIGINS OF HOSTILITY

The first suspicions about converts occurred during the Roman Wars. Roman spies concealed themselves as converts to Judaism, causing the Jewish community to have reason to suspect those who wanted to become Jewish.

When Christianity began growing in size and power, early Christian nations attempted to win all its citizens to the new religion. The Jews were a hold-out people, preferring to remain Jewish.

In order to punish this thorn in its side, the leadership of Christendom made it illegal for a Christian to convert to Judaism. The minimum penalty was loss of all property. More often it was expulsion. England, Spain and Portugal persecuted, then expelled, rabbis who had officiated at conversion ceremonies. In France converts to Judaism and the rabbis who converted them were executed. From 465 C.E. to the end of the Eleventh Century, edicts against Jewish acceptance of converts were enacted by Christian nations on the average of once every sixteen years.

Discretion became the better part of valor, and the Jewish community acquiesed under this pressure. In order to protect the Jewish community from the mass pogroms that were directed against any Jewish village in which a conversion had taken place, converts were discouraged. It is said that this was the cause of the custom of twice rejecting a convert before accepting him as a student. Our antagonism against converts was **imposed on us by outside forces,** and we accepted it as a strategy for survival.

But those days are gone. The laws that were imposed upon us are no longer in force. There is no need to continue responding as though they still had power over us. Why do we persist? I guess it's because when you've been doing something for a thousand years, it becomes a habit.

A HABIT!

Our opposition to converts to Judaism is a habit. A bad habit. And it is high time that we kicked the habit. Our response should be to Jewish mandate, not to antiquated non-Jewish demands imposed upon us.

The convert to Judaism is a first class citizen. In the *Midrash* we find:

> Reish Lakesh said: "The proselyte who converts is dearer than Israel was when she stood before Mount Sinai. Why? Because, had (Israel) not seen the thunder and the lightning and the mountains quaking and the sound of the horns, (the Jewish people) would not have accepted the Torah. But this one, who saw none of those things, came, surrendered himself to the Holy One, and accepted upon himself the Kingdom of Heaven. Could any be dearer than he?"
> —*Midrash Tanhuma, Numbers Rabba, Lech L'cha 6*

The convert shares all the obligations and travails of the Jewish community. He shares, too, in its blessings and *simchas*. When one converts to Judaism, a Hebrew name is given. The first name varies, but most common is *"Avraham"* for men and *"Rut"* for women. Significantly, however, the full name would be *"Avraham Ben Avraham Avinu"* (Abraham son of Abraham the Patriarch) or *"Rut Bat Avraham Avinu"* (Ruth daughter of Abraham the Patriarch). In place of the customary father's name, our tradition bestows upon the convert the parentage of Abraham, the first Jew. By doing so, we are, in effect, saying, "You enter Judaism not in this current date and time. You enter Judaism as every other Jew does—from the time of Abraham the Patriarch. Our history is your history." It is a form of naturalization.

The convert to Judaism is considered a bone fide Jew in every respect. In fact, tradition forbids us from ever referring to the convert as a convert after the conversion has taken place.

TODAY IN THE UNITED STATES

Many American Jews are unaware of the large numbers of those who convert to Judaism every year in the United States. Not only do most rabbis have their own conversion programs, but in the larger cities formal conversion programs are held on a city-wide basis. In most cases prospective converts find their way to the rabbis and conversion programs with little help from the Jewish community. The existence of a dynamic program for converting to Judaism is one of the American Jewish community's best kept secrets.

There are also some small organizations that would go a step further and actively seek out converts. The oldest of these is now based in Los Angeles, the National Jewish Information Service. The newest is the National Jewish Hospitality Committee, based in Philadelphia. There are several others. Their membership and support range from those who would only make literature available in some public way to those who seek to actively engage in proselytizing activity.

Even mainline Jewish organizations like the Union of American Hebrew Congregations has a booklet entitled "How to Become a Jew."

Most American Jews are totally unaware of the thousands who choose Judaism. Our community only knows of the famous individuals who convert to Judaism, such as Sammy Davis, Jr., Elizabeth Taylor, or the late Marilyn Monroe. Most American Jews share a deeply felt fear: Can the convert **really** be a Jew? Can he or she really absorb the culture and heritage of the Jewish people?

Yes, it can be done—if the conversion process is handled correctly.

Recently I received a telephone call from a former student who had been converted some years ago. She was distressed, and in her frustration was calling across 1,500 miles to seek advice. Her husband, who was born Jewish, was making a mockery of her attempts to keep a kosher home. He was rebelling against *kashrut*, and she, a convert, was unable to eat *treif* food. Observance of the dietary laws had become an essential part of her very being.

A PRACTICAL REASON

Not only does tradition allow us to warmly receive those who would voluntarily join us, but there is another reason we should gladly accept converts to Judaism. The Jewish population is dwindling. In this day of uncontrolled world population growth, the Jewish people alone is practicing Zero Population Growth.

Thirty years ago the Nazi Holocaust annihilated one-third of the world's Jewish population. Today we are losing numbers to assimilation, the shift toward smaller families, and—to rejection of prospective converts.

Intermarriage can go either way. We can reject the couple and add one more to the myriad of lost Jews. Or we can embrace the prospective convert with open arms. accepting this as a legitimate opportunity to increase our numbers.

I am not advocating that we engage in missionary activities. Not at all. I am suggesting, though, that when your child announces a pending marriage to a non Jew, **your primary objective as a parent ought to be the creation of an atmosphere that will encourage the non-Jew to join the Jewish people.**

PARENTAL INFLUENCE

As a parent in an intermarriage situation, you are in an awkward role. Some spheres of influence are closed to you; you cannot successfully stop the marriage, nor can you demand that the non-Jew become a convert. **Any** demand you make at this stage might well be used as a test of the couple's loyalty to each other—backfiring in your face.

Making demands will probably be counter-productive. But there is still an influence that you can exert. If the couple is definitely going to be wed, your prime objective ought to be the encouragement of the non-Jew to become a Jew. This can be much simpler than you might realize.

Step 1

First, accept your future son- (daughter-) in-law and let him know that you care about him. Invite the couple to your home to share rituals (e.g. *Shabbat* meal, Passover *seder)* and to go with you to synagogue. The greatest obstacle is the non-Jew's feeling that he is not wanted by his future in-laws. When the non-Jew feels at home with you, you will be in a position to move to the next step.

Step 2

The second step ought to be a discussion of some of the problems the couple will encounter if the marriage is an intermarriage. If you have built a foundation of trust and acceptance (not necessarily approval), the dialogue ought to be amiable and productive.

Step 3

The third step is to suggest to the non-Jew that he **consider the possibility** of conversion to Judaism. Even if the non-Jew does not plan to convert, he will want to know something about Judaism, the religion of his spouse-to-be. If it is approached in a low keyed manner, the non-Jew can be encouraged to attend a course in basic Judaism just to learn about Judaism. Emphasize that no commitments are being asked of him. Without the pressure of a "shotgun conversion" hanging over his head, the non-Jew will in all likelihood agree to take a course in Judaism with a rabbi.

Step 4

The next step is to make certain that the rabbi to whom the non-Jew goes is sympathetic with your family's situation and would encourage conversion during the course of study.

Step 5

Finally, during the time that the non-Jew (and hopefully your child as well) attends the Judaism course, you should have as much contact with the couple as possible, encouraging and supporting them in the difficult decision they must make. As the non-Jew begins to feel a part of a Jewish family, the difficulty of the decision will dissipate, and he will move firmly into the fold of the Jewish people.

8

A Conversion Program

*** The active committee chairperson of Hadassah is not Jewish. She is a non-Jew who has infiltrated that organization.

*** The leader of weekly Israeli dancing at Hillel is not a Jew. She has successfully infiltrated Hillel.

*** An active worker for the United Jewish Appeal has been offered an *aliyah*, to go up to the *Torah*, during a service at a local synagogue. He refuses with some manufactured excuse. He knows that he cannot accept the honor because he is not a Jew.—But only he and his rabbi know this.

These are the daily occurrences in a relatively new program for converts to Judaism—one that uses deception in order to find honesty. It has developed as a solution to the problems confronting people who are in the process of conversion to Judaism. The problems are many and varied. The person studying to become a Jew is undergoing a complete change of identity and self-image. He is being brought into a new family, a new people with its own language, culture, and rituals. He is constantly confronting the mind of the Jew, attempting daily to internalize what he encounters. He must learn, understand and become a part of the entire history of the Jewish people. He must develop a new way of thinking, so that he reacts instinctively when confronted with the Jewish community's emotional concerns: the State of Israel, the memory of the Holocaust, ever present anti-Semitism. It is, indeed, difficult and demanding.

In addition to the problems faced by the convert, others face challenges during this period. The spouse-to-be faces the problem of daily confrontation with his own heritage in light of his loved one's growing into Judaism. The non-Jewish parents of the convert who "lose" their child in a very real sense (as well as *halachicly*) often face their problem without support. The Jewish parents of a native Jew about to marry a convert have a problem in accepting the son-, or daughter-, in-law as really Jewish. Sometimes the rabbi presents a problem; some rabbis discourage prospective converts (See Chapter 7). Other rabbis accept conversion students reluctantly. I think the rabbi ought to *want* to make a Jew out of the conversion student and lend him the kind of support and guidance that will help him in every possible way.

THE QUICKIE CONVERSION . . .

Regardless of the difficulties facing the prospective convert, a significant number have the fortitude and perseverance to complete the requirements and become Jews. As all converts and many born Jews know, each individual rabbi is autonomous in his standards for conversion. In a medium sized city it is not unusual to find a dozen different standards and programs designed for those who wish to convert to Judaism. Sadly, a large number are what might be called "quickie conversions."

A couple comes to a rabbi and asks him to perform a conversion and a wedding. The date of the wedding has already been set. The rabbi, unwilling to officiate at an intermarriage (where one remains non-Jewish), agrees to convert the non-Jew virtually on the spot in order that the wedding can be a Jewish one. This leads to many abuses. Often the student is given a few books to read, has a few sessions with the rabbi, and then proceeds to the conversion ceremony. Although the ritual may be complete and the convert is officially Jewish, the process of internalization—of truly becoming Jewish on the inside—doesn't take place.

...AND THE REAL THING

Fortunately, a growing number of rabbis have begun intensifying their conversion programs and have begun to deal with the situation as a process that must be carefully monitored. The program that I developed some five years ago meets the objective of the convert slowly developing through a process that leads to an internalizing of his Jewish identity. In some ways it is a difficult program; it demands much of the prospective convert. But the difficulty is not meant to be a barrier. On the contrary, most prospective converts are fully aware of the magnitude of the task they have undertaken, and find relief in the fact that there is a highly structured program through which they will be supportively guided.

This program, which normally takes about one year to complete, combines three aspects:

(1) **Academic:** in which he learns about Judaism.

(2) **Counseling:** in which he grapples with the emotional elements of becoming a Jew. And

(3) **Internalizing:** in which he begins to "feel" Jewish.

The program takes a full year for two reasons. First, it takes about that long to assimilate all the data and information about Judaism that one needs to make an educated decision to convert. No commitment of any kind is asked for or accepted until the conversion student has completed the course and wishes to be a candidate for conversion. The second reason the program is designed for a full year is to enable the student to live like a Jew, observing all the Jewish holidays. It is sad, at best, for a convert to Judaism to have never attended a *seder* or a High Holy Day service.

The "Number One Rule" of this program is that if the conversion student is planning to marry a Jew, the spouse-to-be **must** attend the entire program with the prospective convert. It's awfully embarrassing for a convert to live with a native Jew who knows less about Judaism than he does. In many cases the spouse-to-be has been living a marginal Jewish life, and the conversion process actually brings about the "conversion" of two Jews. In most cases

79

the native Jew, experiencing the conversion program with an intended spouse, discovers renewed meaning in Jewish identity.

THE PROGRAM: ACADEMIC ASPECTS

The first part of the conversion program is academic. Conversion students study for a full year. The first semester they attend a course in Basic Judaism which includes:

The Jewish People

The High Holy Days

The Three Festivals: *Sukkot, Pesach* and *Shavuot*

The Holidays of *Chanuka* and *Purim*

Shabbat

The Jewish Bible

The Jewish View of God

Jewish Worship and and the Structure of the Service

The Synagogue

The Jewish Home

The Jewish View of Jesus

The Holocaust

Orthodox, Conservative, Reform and Reconstructionist Movements

The Jewish Attitude Towards Life

The Life Cycle Events

Israel, Zionism and the American Jew

The Jewish Legal System and the *Talmud.*

The students are required to read five basic text books during this semester course.

During the second half of the year, the student, with my approval, selects one aspect of Judaism and concentrates his reading in independent study. Some students, with an affinity for art, have chosen to study Jewish art and archaeology. Some have chosen to specialize in the holidays or in an aspect of Jewish history. Several have chosen political or sociological themes centered around the State of Israel. One law student spent the semester comparing secular law and Jewish tort law. The student may emerge from the conversion program more "learned" than many native Jews, for he has obtained the basics and then concentrated his time in the area of his choice and interest.

At the end of the year the student must go through two examinations. The first is with me. Only after I am satisfied, the student is presented to the *beit din,* the rabbinical court, where he must answer any question posed by the three rabbis. A listing of questions to which answers are expected is found in the next chapter.

This academic program is styled for students at a college or university who are already undergoing the rigors of higher education. The "semester system" and the concept of choosing "electives" and working on "independent study" promotes a sense of familiarity of form while enabling students to reach a level of intellectual achievement similar to that experienced in their secular studies.

THE PROGRAM: COUNSELING

Up until five years ago I carried on weekly counseling sessions with each conversion student individually. But as the number of conversion students grew, I found that meeting with twenty students or couples (as it sometimes occurred) for an hour each week was impossible. Upon the advice of my wife, a social group worker, I instead formed a group counseling session (which I affectionately call the "C-Group") that meets for one-and-a-half hours each week.

The C-Group provides much needed interaction missing from individual counseling sessions. Students who have been working with me for almost a year are helpful—much more than I—with the problems encountered by a new student. A beginning conversion student can immediately identify with someone who has been through similar struggles and who has successfully resolved the problems at hand. No matter how much I might try to empathize with the prospective convert, I cannot really know his innermost feelings; I have never stood where he now stands. Another student, more advanced than he, might respond to a stated anxiety with: "Oh yes, that's the way I felt last fall. When I encountered that situation the first time, I . . ."

The first time a conversion student attends a Jewish worship service—not as a visitor, but as one trying to take part—it can be a frightening experience. Being invited to a *bar mitzvah* or a *seder* for the first time can create anxiety on the part of an outsider.

Knowing "how to break the news" to the gentile parents of the conversion student or the Jewish parents of the spouse-to-be can be traumatic; but terrors are relieved by hearing the experiences of others who have gone through those same confrontations.

Sometimes a veteran will, in response to a newcomer's anxiety, offer to escort the new person to some activity in the Jewish community he may be attending for the first time.

Although the group has done many things for its members, the C-Group has been most helpful with two basic kinds of problems.

First, it confronts difficulties encountered by the conversion student because of parents. Sometimes the problem revolves around the convert's parents. But more likely it is due to the Jewish parents-in-law-to-be who cannot accept a convert (especially one who will marry THEIR child) as a Jew. The mere assurance by others who have been through this nightmare can help relieve a new student.

The second area of help is theological. Most prospective converts whom I see have long ago given up their childhood religions; now they must go through a painful process of trying to understand, believe, feel and know the God of the Jews. The worship experience is often alien to them; the Hebrew language, the concepts and the form are different from their past experience. At first, many feel they cannot cope. They sometimes find themselves overwhelmed by the style of worship, the intellectual thrust of sermons, the familial relationship to God, the lack of decorum (in some services), the relatively large number of prayers connected with the land of Israel, and the strong sense of community.

The concerns of the students are deeply felt. Yet they find themselves capable of opening up and exposing themselves within the group. When a problem is expressed, several group members respond with their own experiences, feelings, suggestions and concerns. The encouragement that one conversion student can give another is often needed throughout the stages of the conversion process.

Converting to Judaism is like walking across a bridge. The conversion student has left one bank behind and has not yet arrived on the other. Somewhere out there in the middle, the feeling of loneliness can become overpowering. In the C-Group conversion students gain support and friendship as well as the all-important knowledge that they are not alone in this difficult transitional period.

In addition to the C-Group, individual counseling with conversion students is also available. For some, it comes rarely—when something arises which a student thinks is too personal to discuss in the group. For others, the need to meet individually with the rabbi is felt fairly often. Each student's needs are different.

THE PROGRAM: PASSING

Conversion students are told at the very beginning that becoming a Jew is not just accepting certain stated beliefs or dogmas. We have beliefs, yes, and we have *mitzvot,* commandments, too. But essentially, to become a Jew is to become a member of the Jewish people, accepting as one's very own the history, the heritage, the culture, the mind-set, as well as the religion of Jews. Reading books and discussing them with a rabbi is not sufficient. There remains a crucial hiatus in one's self-image as a Jew. Most conversion programs consist of the academic and counseling components, dealing with the heart and the mind. The third segment of this conversion program deals with the soul, the internalization of Jewish consciousness.

I tell prospective converts to think of a woman who sees a dress advertised for sale in a store. She goes to the store, sees the dress on a manniquin in the window, but first goes down the street to see what the competition is selling. Then she returns to the store, goes in, takes the same dress—and two others—and tries on all three. She then purchases the dress she planned to buy all along. . . . But it is only after she gets home and tries it on in the intimacy of her home that she is truly convinced that she has done the right thing.

I ask conversion students to treat Judaism as earnestly as the woman in the illustration. Because it is really rather more like buying a bathing suit; once you have bought it, you cannot return it.

In order to "try on the dress," the student is told that from the moment he leaves my office at the end of the very first interview, he is to "think Jewish." The student is told to outwardly identify himself as a Jew—not as a convert, nor as a conversion student, but as a Jew—to one and all. Some wear obvious identifying jewelry; others impart this information in conversations. For one year each conversion student is to live like a Jew, celebrating the Jewish holidays and *Shabbat*, participating in all levels of the Jewish community, feeling like a Jew in a non-Jewish world.

Some conversion students become involved in Hillel; their identities are not known to other Hillel students. Others become involved in synagogues and Jewish organizations. They find out **before conversion** the day-to-day reality of being a Jew. They discover the difficulties of being in a minority in a Christian/secular culture. But more poignantly, they are exposed to internal Jewish bigotry from which they would have been sheltered if they were known as converts.

One of my conversion students was told in confidence by someone unsuspecting of her identity: "The President of the Sisterhood is a *shikse!*" Naively, the student asked, "How can a *shikse* be President of the Sisterhood?" The response: "Oh, she converted years ago, but you know what those converts are like!"

Living as Jews, passing as a Jew with other Jews—this is the single most crucial element in making the difficult transition from gentile to Jew. In combination with this internalizing component, the time spent in study and counseling is used more effectively.

"A demanding conversion program," you say. Yes! But a demanding conversion course is not the same as a discouraging one. Most of the students with whom I have worked have found the highly structured program helpful. And I believe that we need to be more helpful to those who would join with us.

OPENNESS TO CONVERSION

Our tradition is the most consistent with those values society needs the most. The dream of Messianic fulfillment gives hope in an age of fear. The centrality of the Jewish family can be a bulwark against the collapse of the American family structure. The Jew's concern for his fellowmen is undiminished while secular society becomes more remote from the plight of the less fortunate. Judaism is a religion blending mysticism with reason, where the questioning Jew is the pious Jew. For the thinking, Twentieth Century person, Judaism can represent a challenging, yet supportive basis from which to confront the problems of the day.

In our society today there are many thinking people who are searching for the kind of life that only Judaism can provide.

When a Jew plans to marry a non-Jew, our goal ought to be an ingathering, a bringing back of the Jew and the offering of a welcoming hand to the non-Jew. We need to invite him to share our heritage and our dream for the future.

9

Questions A Convert Must Answer

There are three kinds of questions that are usually asked of converts during the process of the *beit din* (rabbinical court). They are as follows:

(1) Easy questions,
(2) Difficult questions, and
(3) Impossible questions.

The **impossible questions** are those for which the prospective convert cannot study. They deal with his sincerity and feelings. They are questions such as:

"Why do you want to be a Jew?"

"Do you really feel Jewish? How?"

The **difficult questions** are those that force the prospective convert to synthesize information that he or she has learned, such as:

"What is the basic thrust of Jewish history in the early post-emancipation period?"

"How does a contemporary Jew relate to the Holocaust? How do you feel about it?"

"What is the role of the State of Israel to an American Jew?"

The **easy questions** are straight-forward and direct. They are asked from a list that the student is given in the beginning of his studies. These questions cover many areas and can be answered as briefly or in as much detail as the individual desires. The list I use is as follows:

1 The Jewish People

1. What is a Jew?
2. Are we a nation, race, religion or nationality?
3. What is the Jewish attitude toward proselytes (converts)?
4. What is the Jewish attitude toward proselytizing missionary activity?
5. Explain the basic differences between Orthodox, Conservative, Reform and Reconstructionist Judaism.
6. Is the existence of different branches of Judaism consistent with our past? Explain.
7. Identify and explain the following terms:
   (1) Saducees
   (2) Pharisees
   (3) *Hasidim*
   (4) *Mitnagdim*
   (5) *Beit Din*
   (6) Karaites
   (7) *K'lal Yisrael*

2 The Jewish View of God and Prayer

1. What is "The Watchword of our Faith" and what does it mean?
2. What does Judaism require us to believe about God?
3. Explain the various views of God that Jewish philosophers have held in various ages.
4. What does the Hebrew word for "prayer" mean?
5. What are the basic prayers that make up the Jewish worship service?
6. How old are some of the prayers?
7. How does Judaism feel about communal worship?

8. What is the prayer for the following?
   (1) Wine
   (2) Sabbath candles
   (3) Holiday candles
   (4) Before meals
   (5) After meals
   (6) Joyous occasions
9. Identify and explain the following terms:
   (1) *Minyan*
   (2) *Elohim*
   (3) *Elohenu*
   (4) *Adonai*
   (5) *L'hitpalel*

3   The Jewish Bible

1. What is the Hebrew name for the Bible?
2. What is the Jewish Bible?
3. When was the Bible written and by whom?
4. What does the word *"Torah"* mean?
5. Is the Bible true?
6. Identify and explain the following terms:
   (1) *Apocrypha*
   (2) *Tanach*
   (3) *N'vee-eem*
   (4) *K'tuveem*

4   The High Holy Days

1. How long is the High Holy Day period and what is its significance?
2. What is the Jewish view of repentance and atonement?
3. How should a Jew observe *Rosh Hashana* and *Yom Kippur?*
4. Identify and explain the following terms:
   (1) *Rosh Hashana*
   (2) *Yom Kippur*
   (3) *Shabbat Shuva*
   (4) *Shofar*
   (5) *Kol Nidre*

5   The Three Festivals

1. Name the Three Jewish Festivals.

2. What is the origin of each?
3. When are each of them observed?
4. What is the religious, agricultural and historical significance of each of them?
5. How does a Jew observe each of the Three Festivals?
6. Identify and explain the following terms:
    (1) *Sukkot*
    (2) *Pesach*
    (3) *Shavuot*
    (4) *Etrog*
    (5) *Lulav*
    (6) *Seder*
    (7) *Matzah*
    (8) *Charoset*
    (9) *Chazeret*
    (10) *Z'rua*
    (11) *Maror*
    (12) *Karpais*
    (13) *Haggadah*
    (14) *Simchat Torah*

6 The Holiday of *Purim*

1. What is the origin of the holiday of *Purim?*
2. How do we celebrate *Purim?*
3. What is the religious significance of *Purim?*
4. Identify and explain the following terms:
    (1) *Greggar*
    (2) *Hamantaschen*
    (3) *Megilla*
    (4) *Sh'lach manot*

7 The Sabbath

1. What is the meaning of the Sabbath?
2. What is the significance of the *Torah* and the *Haftara* portions?
3. What is the *Havdala* ceremony?
4. How do Jews observe the Sabbath?
5. What is the relationship between the Jewish Sabbath and the Christian Sunday?
6. Identify and explain the following terms:
    (1) *Challa*

(2) *"Shabbat Shalom"*
(3) *Kiddush*

8 The Synagogue and the Home

1. Trace briefly the early development of the synagogue.
2. What is the three-fold purpose of the synagogue?
3. How is a contemporary synagogue governed?
4. What is the role of a rabbi in a synagogue?
5. Describe the major ritual objects found in the sanctuary.
6. Explain the place of the home in the practice and preservation of Judaism.
7. What is the significance of the *mezuzah* on the door?
8. Identify and explain the following terms:
    (1) *Aron Hakodesh*
    (2) *Ner Tamid*
    (3) *Bima*
    (4) *Menorah*
    (5) *Siddur*
    (6) *Machzor*
    (7) *Shul*
    (8) *Tallit*
    (9) *Kipa*
    (10) *Tefillin*

9 The Holiday of *Chanuka*

1. Explain the origin and development of *Chanuka.*
2. What is the relationship between *Chanuka* and Christmas?
3. What is the religious significance of *Chanuka?*
4. *Identify and explain the following terms:*
    (1) *Maccabees*
    (2) *Chanukiah (sic)*
    (3) *Shamash*
    (4) *Dreydel*

10 The Jewish Attitude Toward Jesus

1. Who was the historical Jesus?
2. Who was responsible for the death of Jesus?
3. How did Jesus fit into the developing Messianic concept?
4. How did Paul reinforce this concept?
5. What are modern Jewish and Christian views about the Messiah?

6. What is the difference between "Jesus" and "Christ"?

11 Modern Movements in Judaism

1. Where did Reform Judaism begin and why did it fail there?
2. How and why did Conservative Judaism begin?
3. What is Reconstructionist Judaism and how did it develop?
4. Describe modern Orthodox Judaism.
5. Who are the *Hasidim?*
6. What is "The Historical School of Judaism?"
7. What Reform innovations have been adopted by other branches of Judaism?
8. Identify and explain the following terms:
    (1) Isaac Leeser
    (2) Mordecai M. Kaplan
    (3) Isaac Mayer Wise
    (4) Stephen S. Wise
    (5) Solomon Schechter
    (6) Union of Orthodox Jewish Congregations of America
    (7) Rabbinical Council of America
    (8) Yeshiva University
    (9) Isaac Elchanan Rabbinical School
    (10) United Synagogue of America
    (11) The Rabbinical Assembly
    (12) Hebrew Union College—Jewish Institute of Religion
    (13) Union of American Hebrew Congregations
    (14) Central Conference of American Rabbis
    (15) Federation of Reconstructionist Congregations and Fellowships
    (16) Reconstructionist Rabbinical College
    (17) Reconstructionist Rabbinical Association

12 The Jewish Attitude Toward Life

1. How does Judaism look upon "original sin?"
2. What is the Jewish view of humanity?
3. What was Hillel's rule of conduct toward others?
4. What is the Jewish view of suicide?
5. What is the Jewish view of abortion and birth control?
6. What role does *Kashrut* play in Judaism?
7. What do Jews believe about afterlife, salvation and the soul?
8. What is the Jewish view of sin?

9. Identify and explain the following terms:
   (1) *Olam haba*
   (2) *Kosher*
   (3) *Treif*
   (4) *Milchig*
   (5) *Fleishig*

13   The Life Cycle Ceremonies

1. What ceremony is performed for a newly born Jewish boy?
2. When does it take place? What is its significance?
3. What is the ceremony for a girl's birth?
4. What is involved in a Jewish wedding ceremony?
5. What is the Jewish attitude toward divorce?
6. What is the Jewish custom of mourning?
7. Identify and explain the following terms:
   (1) *B'rit*
   (2) Consecration
   (3) Confirmation
   (4) *Bar Mitzvah*
   (5) *Bat Mitzvah*
   (6) *Kiddushin*
   (7) *Yahrzeit*
   (8) *Kaddish*

14   The *Talmud* and Jewish Law

1. What is the *Midrash?* When was it written?
2. Tell something about its contents.
3. What is the *Talmud?* When was it written?
4. Tell something about its contents.
5. What are the differences between the Jerusalem *Talmud* and the Babylonian *Talmud?*
6. What is the Written Law and the Oral Law?
7. How do traditional and liberal Jews feel about them?
8. In what languages was the *Talmud* written?
9. What is the concept of *"mitzvah"* in Rabbinic Judaism?
10. Identify and explain the following terms:
    (1) *Halacha*
    (2) *Aggada*
    (3) *Mishnah*
    (4) *Gemara*

(5) *Responsa*

(6) *Shulchan Auruch*

15 The Holocaust

1. What were the various stages of Nazi anti-Jewish persecution?
2. What really happened to European Jewry during the Holocaust?
3. How did the world respond to the Holocaust?
4. How has the Holocaust affected Jewish attitudes toward non-Jews?
5. Identify and explain the following terms:
   (1) Auschwitz
   (2) Treblinka
   (3) "614th Commandment"
   (4) Nuremberg Laws
   (5) *Kristallnacht*
   (6) Shoah
   (7) "The Final Solution"
   (8) The Warsaw Ghetto

16 Israel and Zionism

1. What is the biblical background of the Jewish people's connection with the land of Israel?
2. When did political Zionism begin? Why? By whom?
3. What was the role of the United Nations in establishing the State of Israel?
4. What has been its role since then?
5. What are the basic facts of the ongoing Israeli-Arab dispute?
6. What place does Israel have in the life of an American Jew?
7. Identify and explain the following terms:
   (1) Balfour Declaration
   (2) Jewish National Fund
   (3) Chaim Weizmann
   (4) Theodor Herzl
   (5) David Ben Gurion
   (6) *Aliyah Bet*
   (7) Paris Peace Conference of 1919
   (8) *Knesset*
   (9) *Eretz Yisrael*

(10) Menahem Begin
(11) *Sabra*
(12) *Galut*

10

The Ritual of Conversion

Because conversion is such a personal rite, the majority of Jews have never had an opportunity to participate in or witness one. As a result, the "unknown" quality of the ritual has created a mystique. In reality, the conversion ceremony ought to be known and understood by all Jews, for it is one of the most beautiful and significant rites in Judaism.

The common practice is for the convert to meet with the three rabbis of the *beit din* privately. In some cases the spouse-to-be is also invited to attend the questioning session. (The *b'rit* and *mikveh,* which will be explained later, are limited to the convert and the minimum number of required witnesses.) When all of the requirements have been met, it is customary for the convert and the rabbis to then go inside the synagogue sanctuary and conduct the formal ceremony before the open Ark. Again, even this ceremony is private and is attended usually only by the spouse-to-be.

Some converts, however, may find differing procedures. For example, sometimes the actual conversion ceremony is held publicly before the congregation during a Friday night service. In this way the congregation shares with the convert his process of formalizing the relationship with Judaism.

There is no set time for the conversion ceremony to be held. It is at the discretion of the officiating rabbi and the convert to select a mutually acceptable day and time.

This is the step-by-step procedure of the conversion ritual:

The *B'rit*

A male Jew must be circumcised. Even though a male convert has already been circumcised, it does not count according to Jewish law as his having entered the convenant (b'rit). *Each male Jewish child enters the convenant with circumcision on his eighth day. A convert, too, must go through this ritual. However, re-doing a circumcision is physically impossible, so a substitute ritual called* "hatofat hadam" *(drop of blood) was developed. In this ritual, one drop of blood is taken from the penis of the male convert in the presence of two male witnesses. Though this procedure is simple and could be performed by anyone, normally a male Jewish physician extracts the single drop of blood—not because it is complicated, but to insure that it will remain a simple matter. This fulfills the requirement and is physiologically (if not psychologically) of little note.*

The Reform movement does not require a circumcised male convert to undergo hatofat hadam.

Mikveh

Following the questioning by the rabbis and hatofat hadam *(for male converts), the next step is* t'vila, *immersion in a* mikveh—*in a body of "living water" such as a river or an indoor* mikveh *containing some rain water.*

The convert must totally disrobe, removing all clothing and jewelry while a Jewish witness of the same sex, chosen by the officiating rabbi, observes the immersion. (The convert should find out in advance whether it is necessary to bring a towel as it becomes somewhat awkward when they are not provided.)

In some cities there is no mikveh *available and public bodies of water must be used. In Miami, Florida, for example, where the existing* mikveh *does not allow non-Orthodox rabbis to officiate, the Reform and Conservative communities have developed the following compromise: The immersion takes place at a beach where the convert wears a loosely-fitting bathing suit (not a bikini!). In this way the water touches all parts of the body.*

The Reform movement does not require t'vila; nevertheless, many Reform rabbis ask their conversion students to participate in this part of the ritual.

The convert recites the following blessings, then immerses himself completely three times:

בָּרוּךְ אַתָּה יְיָ אֱלֹהֵינוּ מֶלֶךְ הָעוֹלָם, אֲשֶׁר קִדְּשָׁנוּ בְּמִצְוֹתָיו
וְצִוָּנוּ עַל הַטְּבִילָה.

בָּרוּךְ אַתָּה יְיָ אֱלֹהֵינוּ מֶלֶךְ הָעוֹלָם, שֶׁהֶחֱיָנוּ וְקִיְּמָנוּ וְהִגִּיעָנוּ
לַזְּמַן הַזֶּה.

Praised are You, O Lord our God, Ruler of the universe, Who has sanctified us with Your commandments and commanded us concerning immersion.

Praised are You, O Lord our God, Ruler of the universe, Who has granted us life, sustained us, and has brought us to this moment.

Sometimes, following the immersion, the rabbi will read from Ezekiel 36:

With pure water I will cleanse you, and you shall be clean; from all your impurities will I cleanse you. A new heart will I give you, and a new spirit will I put within you. I will cause you to follow My teachings, and you shall keep My statues. You shall be My people, and I will be your God.

Introductory Prayers

Following the immersion, the convert dries off (often bringing a hair drier with him) and dresses. Then the convert joins the rabbis as they procede into the sanctuary to stand before the Ark. It is at this point that the spouse-to-be usually joins the ceremony.

The rabbi (the member of the beit din *who has worked most closely with the convert usually reads the parts assigned to "the rabbi") reads one of several introductory prayers which bless God, express gratitude, ask God's continual help and guidance, and pray that the convert will find satisfaction in his newly chosen life.*

99

The Charge

The rabbi delivers the charge—personal words to the convert.

Declaration of Faith

In some ceremonies the convert will be asked to read a declaration of faith, stating voluntary desire to become a part of the Jewish people, hoping to be worthy of the commitment, and declaring a determination to have a Jewish home and raise his or her children as Jews.

In other ceremonies the convert will be asked to respond to several questions posed by the rabbi. These questions will deal with the volunatary nature of the commitment, the severance of ties to former religions, the pledge of loyalty to the Jewish people in times of persecution as well as in times of freedom, and the promise to have a Jewish home and raise children as Jews.

The *Shema*

The Shema, *"the watchword of our faith,"* is the extreme statement of monotheism. The convert will be asked to read all or part of the following in Hebrew and/or English:

שְׁמַע יִשְׂרָאֵל יְיָ אֱלֹהֵינוּ יְיָ אֶחָד.

בָּרוּךְ שֵׁם כְּבוֹד מַלְכוּתוֹ לְעוֹלָם וָעֶד.

וְאָהַבְתָּ אֵת יְהוָֹה אֱלֹהֶיךָ בְּכָל־לְבָבְךָ וּבְכָל־נַפְשְׁךָ
וּבְכָל־מְאֹדֶךָ. וְהָיוּ הַדְּבָרִים הָאֵלֶּה, אֲשֶׁר אָנֹכִי מְצַוְּךָ הַיּוֹם,
עַל־לְבָבֶךָ. וְשִׁנַּנְתָּם לְבָנֶיךָ, וְדִבַּרְתָּ בָּם בְּשִׁבְתְּךָ בְּבֵיתֶךָ,
וּבְלֶכְתְּךָ בַדֶּרֶךְ, וּבְשָׁכְבְּךָ וּבְקוּמֶךָ. וּקְשַׁרְתָּם לְאוֹת עַל־יָדֶךָ,
וְהָיוּ לְטֹטָפֹת בֵּין עֵינֶיךָ. וּכְתַבְתָּם עַל־מְזֻזוֹת בֵּיתֶךָ וּבִשְׁעָרֶיךָ.
לְמַעַן תִּזְכְּרוּ וַעֲשִׂיתֶם אֶת־כָּל־מִצְוֹתָי, וִהְיִיתֶם קְדֹשִׁים
לֵאלֹהֵיכֶם.

Hear, O Israel, the Lord our God, the Lord is one.
Praised is His name whose glorious Kingdom is forever and ever.

You shall love the Lord with all your heart, with all your soul, and with all your might. These words, which I command you this day, shall be in your heart. You shall teach them diligently to your children. You shall talk about them when you are at home and when you are away, when you lie down and when you rise up. You shall bind them for a sign on your hand, and they shall be as frontlets between your eyes. And you shall write them upon the doorposts of your house and on your gates. Then will you remember and do all My commandments, and be holy before your God.

The Book of Ruth

In most conversion ceremonies the convert then reads the section of Scripture that refers to Ruth's conversion:

And Ruth said, "Entreat me not to leave you, and to turn away from following you. For where you go, I will go, and where you lodge, I will lodge. Your people will be my people, and your God my God. Where you die, will I die, and there will I be buried. I solemnly swear before the Lord that nothing but death will part you and me."

—Ruth 1:16-17

Alenu

The rabbi reads:

עָלֵינוּ לְשַׁבֵּחַ לַאֲדוֹן הַכֹּל, לָתֵת גְּדֻלָּה לְיוֹצֵר בְּרֵאשִׁית, שֶׁלֹּא
עָשֶׂנוּ כְּגוֹיֵי הָאֲרָצוֹת, וְלֹא שָׂמְנוּ כְּמִשְׁפְּחוֹת הָאֲדָמָה, שֶׁלֹּא
שָׂם חֶלְקֵנוּ כָּהֶם, וְגֹרָלֵנוּ כְּכָל־הֲמוֹנָם. וַאֲנַחְנוּ כּוֹרְעִים
וּמִשְׁתַּחֲוִים וּמוֹדִים לִפְנֵי מֶלֶךְ מַלְכֵי הַמְּלָכִים הַקָּדוֹשׁ בָּרוּךְ
הוּא, שֶׁהוּא נוֹטֶה שָׁמַיִם וְיוֹסֵד אָרֶץ, וּמוֹשַׁב יְקָרוֹ בַּשָּׁמַיִם
מִמַּעַל, וּשְׁכִינַת עֻזּוֹ בְּגָבְהֵי מְרוֹמִים. הוּא אֱלֹהֵינוּ, אֵין עוֹד.
אֱמֶת מַלְכֵּנוּ, אֶפֶס זוּלָתוֹ, כַּכָּתוּב בְּתוֹרָתוֹ: וְיָדַעְתָּ הַיּוֹם
וַהֲשֵׁבֹתָ אֶל־לְבָבֶךָ, כִּי יְיָ הוּא הָאֱלֹהִים בַּשָּׁמַיִם מִמַּעַל וְעַל־
הָאָרֶץ מִתָּחַת, אֵין עוֹד.

עַל־כֵּן נְקַוֶּה לְךָ, יְיָ אֱלֹהֵינוּ, לִרְאוֹת מְהֵרָה בְּתִפְאֶרֶת
עֻזֶּךָ, לְהַעֲבִיר גִּלּוּלִים מִן־הָאָרֶץ, וְהָאֱלִילִים כָּרוֹת יִכָּרֵתוּן,
לְתַקֵּן עוֹלָם בְּמַלְכוּת שַׁדַּי, וְכָל־בְּנֵי בָשָׂר יִקְרְאוּ בִשְׁמֶךָ,
לְהַפְנוֹת אֵלֶיךָ כָּל־רִשְׁעֵי אָרֶץ. יַכִּירוּ וְיֵדְעוּ כָּל־יוֹשְׁבֵי תֵבֵל,
כִּי לְךָ תִכְרַע כָּל־בֶּרֶךְ, תִּשָּׁבַע כָּל־לָשׁוֹן. לְפָנֶיךָ, יְיָ אֱלֹהֵינוּ
יִכְרְעוּ וְיִפֹּלוּ, וְלִכְבוֹד שִׁמְךָ יְקָר יִתֵּנוּ, וִיקַבְּלוּ כֻלָּם אֶת־עֹל
מַלְכוּתֶךָ, וְתִמְלֹךְ עֲלֵיהֶם מְהֵרָה לְעוֹלָם וָעֶד, כִּי הַמַּלְכוּת
שֶׁלְּךָ הִיא, וּלְעוֹלְמֵי עַד תִּמְלֹךְ בְּכָבוֹד, כַּכָּתוּב בְּתוֹרָתֶךָ:
יְיָ יִמְלֹךְ לְעֹלָם וָעֶד. וְנֶאֱמַר: וְהָיָה יְיָ לְמֶלֶךְ עַל־כָּל־הָאָרֶץ,
בַּיּוֹם הַהוּא יִהְיֶה יְיָ אֶחָד וּשְׁמוֹ אֶחָד.

Let us adore the everliving God and render praise unto Him who spread out the heavens and established the earth, whose glory is revealed in the heavens above and whose greatness in manifest throughout the world. He is our God; there is none else.

We bow the head and worship the King of Kings, the Holy One, blessed is He.

May the time come soon, O God, when Your name shall be worshipped throughout the world, when unbelief shall disappear and perfection reign. We pray that the day will come when all humanity will acknowledge You, when corruption and evil will give way to purity and goodness, when superstition shall no longer enslave the mind nor idolatry blind the eye, when everyone shall know that to you alone every knee must bend and every tongue give praise. May all, created in Your image, recognize that they are brothers, so that together they may forever be united before You. Then your Kingdom shall be established on earth, as it is written in the Torah:

"The Lord will reign eternally. On that day the Lord shall be one and his name shall be one."

Conferring the Hebrew Name

The rabbi officially welcomes the convert into the family of the Jewish people by bestowing on him a Hebrew name.

Reading the Certificate

In some ceremonies the conversion certificate is read as part of the ritual. The text of the certificate can be found in this chapter following the ceremony.

The Final Blessing

In Reform conversion ceremonies, the rabbi usually places his hand on the convert and recites:

יְבָרֶכְךָ יְיָ וְיִשְׁמְרֶךָ:

יָאֵר יְיָ פָּנָיו אֵלֶיךָ וִיחֻנֶּךָ:

יִשָּׂא יְיָ פָּנָיו אֵלֶיךָ וְיָשֵׂם לְךָ שָׁלוֹם:

May the Lord bless you and keep you.

May the Lord cause His presence to shine on you and be gracious unto you.

May the Lord lift up His presence upon you and grant you peace. Amen.

The Ceremony is Over

That is the entirety of the conversion ceremony. When it has concluded, it ends as simply as it began. The Ark is closed, and all those participating leave the sanctuary. The convert is now a Jew in every sense.

THE CONVERSION CERTIFICATE

1. Reform Certificate

This is to certify that (name) of (city) came before me, (Rabbi's name) on the (date) of (month and year), corresponding to the Hebrew date (date), expressing (his/her) desire for conversion to the Jewish religion and giving satisfactory evidence that (he/she) knows and understands the principles and practices of Judaism. Therefore, with the sanction of the two associates whose names are signed below, I received the said (name) into the fellowship of the Jewish people and faith, giving (him/her) the additional Hebrew name (name).

On (his/her) part, (name) has solemnly declared (his/her) intention to cast in (his/her) lot with the Jewish people, to live in accordance with the Jewish religion, and if blessed with children, to rear them as Jews.

> Signed: Rabbi
> Two witnesses
> Convert

2. Conservative Certificate

This is to certify that on the (date) day of (month and year in Jewish calendar), corresponding to the (date) day of (month and year in secular calendar), in the city of (name), there came before the undersigned duly constituted *Beit Din* (name of convert), who declared (his/her) desire to enter the covenant of the people of Israel as a righteous proselyte. We questioned (him/her) and found that (he/she) was sincere in (his/her) intention and adequately conversant with the doctrines and practices of Judaism. (He/she) has fulfilled the required ritual(s) of (circumcision and) immersion, as prescribed by Jewish law and tradition.

We therefore declare (him/her) to be truly a member of the Jewish community, and we confer upon (him/her) the name (Hebrew name).

May the God of our father Abraham bless (him/her) and grant (him/her) the strength and courage to abide faithfully and loyally by the precepts and observances of our holy Torah, so that (he/she) may become a worthy member of the House of Israel, chosen by God to bear testimony to His righteousness among all mankind.

Signed in this city of (name) and state of (name) on (date).

Signed: Three rabbis

3. Reconstructionist Certificate

The Reconstructionist movement has not yet developed a standard certificate. The following is a draft currently being considered by the Reconstructionist movement which reflects the philosophy of this movement.*

This is to certify that on the (date) day of (month and year in Jewish calendar), corresponding to the (date) day of (month and year in secular calendar), there came before the undersigned duly constituted *Beit Din* at Congregation (name), (city and state), (name of convert) who declared his/her desire to enter the covenant of the people of Israel as a righteous proselyte. We questioned him/her and found that he/she was sincere in his/her intention and adequately conversant with the principles and practices of Judaism. He/she has, furthermore, fulfilled the rituals prescribed for Proselytes by Jewish law and tradition.

We therefore declare him/her to be truly within the Jewish faith and a full member of the Jewish community, and we confer upon him/her the name of (Hebrew name).

May the God of our ancestors bless him/her and grant him/her the strength and courage to abide faithfully and loyally by the ideals, precepts and observances of our holy Torah tradition, so that he/she may become a worthy member of the House of Israel, which proclaims the uniqueness of God, the unity of humanity and the reign of the law of righteousness.

Signed in this city of (name), State of (name), on (date).

Signed: Three rabbis

---

*This draft was made available by Rabbi Dennis S. Sasso, Chairman of the Commission on Conversion of the Reconstructionist Rabbinical Association.

4. Orthodox Certificate

The Orthodox movement does not utilize a formal certificate. The officiating rabbi writes a document, in his own words, stating that the convert was properly questioned by a constituted beit din, *performed the required rituals, and was admitted into the Jewish people on the specified date in the specified location.*

FOR FURTHER READING

BOOKS

Bamberger, Bernard J. *Proselytism in the Talmudic Period.* New York: Ktav Publishing House, Inc. 1939.

Berman, Louis A. *Jews and Intermarriage.* New York: Thomas Yoseloff. 1968.

Braude, William G. *Jewish Proselytizing.* Providence: Brown University Press. 1940.

Cahnman, Werner J. *Intermarriage and Jewish Life.* New York: Herzl Press. 1963.

Eichhorn, David Max. *Conversion to Judaism: A History and Analysis.* New York: Ktav Publishing House, Inc. 1965.

Eichhorn, David Max. *Jewish Intermarriages: Fact and Fiction.* Satellite Beach, FL: Satellite Books. 1974.

Gordon, A.I. *Intermarriage.* Boston: Beacon Press. 1964.

Peterson, John. *Missionary Methods of Judaism in the Early Roman Empire.* Chicago: University of Chicago Press. 1946.

Sandmel, Samuel. *When a Jew and Christian Marry.* Philadelphia: Fortress Press. 1977.

ARTICLES AND PAMPHLETS

Bubis, Gerald B. "The Sociology of Intermarriage." Los Angeles: Southern California Association of Liberal Rabbis and the Southern California Section of the Rabbinical Assembly. May 1972.

Caven, Ruth S. "Jewish Student Attitudes Toward Interreligious and Intra-Jewish Marriage." *American Journal of Sociology.* Vol. 76, No. 6. May 1971.

Cohen, Henry. "Mixed Marriage and Jewish Continuity." *C.C.A.R. Journal.* Vol. 19, No. 2. April 1972. pp. 48-55.

Davis, Daniel L. "Intermarriage?" New York Federation of Reform Synagogues. n.d.

Eichhorn, David Max. "The Challenge of Intermarriage: The Rabbi's Dilemma." *Congress Bi-Weekly.* March 23, 1964. pp. 7-10.

Eichhorn, David Max. "Conversion for Marriage." *Bamakom.* Vol. 1, No. 3. Spring, 1974. p. 12 ff.

Fein, Leonard. "Some Consequences of Jewish Intermarriage." *Jewish Social Studies.* Vol. 33. 1971. pp. 44-59.

Gendler, Everett. "Identity, Invisible Religion and Intermarriage." *Response.* No. 6, Winter 1969-1970.

Goldstein, Sidney. "American Jewry, 1970: A Demographic Profile." *American Jewish Yearbook.* Vol. 72. New York and Philadelphia: American Jewish Committee and the Jewish Publication Society of America. pp. 3-88. 1972.

Jacobs, Robert P. "The Needs of the Student Convert." *Bamakom.* Vol. 1, No. 3. Spring 1974, p. 8 ff.

Johnson, George E. "Comparing the Inmarried and Intermarried: Implications of the National Jewish Population Study." *Analysis.* No. 32. New York: Institute for Jewish Policy Planning and Research of the Synagogue Council of America. January 15, 1973.

Jung, Leo. "The Challenge of Intermarriage: The Historical View." *Congress Bi-Weekly.* March 23, 1964. pp. 7-10.

Kaplan, Mordecai M. "The Problem of Jewish Interfaith Marriage." Long Beach, NY: Federation of Jewish Philanthropies. December 1964. (From the Nearprint Collection of the American Jewish Archives, Cincinnati.)

Klein, Joseph. "The Challenge of Intermarriage: The Rabbi's Responsibility." *Congress Bi-Weekly.* March 23, 1964. pp. 10-11.

Lazerwitz, B. "Intermarriage and Conversion: A Guide for Future Research." *Jewish Journal of Sociology.* Vol. 13. June 1971. pp. 41-63.

Levinson, M.H. and Levinson, D.J. "Jews Who Intermarry." *YIVO Annual of Social Science.* Vol. 12. 1958-1959.

Maller, Allen S. "Jews and Intermarriage." *Jewish Spectator.* February 1969.

Maller, Allen S. "Marriage: Mixed or Matched." *The National Jewish Monthly.* April 1972. pp. 40-45.

Maller, Allen S. "Mixed Marriage and Reform Rabbis." *Reconstructionist.* November 1972.

Maller, Allen S. "Mixed or Mitzva Marriages." *Jewish Spectator.* Vol. 4, No. 6. p. 8 ff.

Maller, Allen S. "New Facts About Mixed Marriages." *Reconstructionist.* Vol. 23. 1969.

Massarik, Fred, Ed. "National Jewish Population Study: Intermarriage: Facts for Planning." New York: Council of Jewish Federations and Welfare Funds. 1973.

Massarik, Fred. "Rethinking the Intermarriage Crisis." *Moment.* Vol. 3, No. 7. June 1978. pp. 29-33.

Mirsky, Norman B. "Mixed Marriages and the Reform Rabbis." *Midstream.* Vol. 16, No. 1. January 1970.

Polish, David. "The Problem of Intermarriage: Will Moderation Help?" *C.C.A.R. Journal.* January 1964. pp. 33-37.

Rabinowitz, Louis Isaac and Eichhorn, David Max. "Proselytes." *Encyclopedia Judaica.* Vol. 13. pp. 1182-1193. Jerusalem: Keter Publishers. 1972.

Raphael, Marc Lee. "Intermarriage and Jewish Survival: A Hard Disjunction." *C.C.A.R. Journal.* Vol. 19, No. 2. April 1972. pp. 56-61.

Rosenthal, Erich. "Jewish Intermarriage in Indiana." *American Jewish Yearbook.* Vol. 68. New York and Philadelphia: The American Jewish Committee and the Jewish Publication Society of America. 1968.

Rosenthal, Erich. "Studies of Jewish Intermarriage in the United States." *American Jewish Yearbook.* Vol. 64. New York and Philadelphia: The American Jewish Committee and the Jewish Publication Society of America. 1964.

Schereschewsky, Ben-Zion. "Mixed Marriage." *Encyclopedia Judaica.* Vol 12. pp. 164-169. Jerusalem: Keter Publishers. 1972.

Schwartz, Arnold. "Intermarriage in the United States." American Jewish Yearbook. Vol. 71. New York and Philadelphia: The American Jewish Committee and the Jewish Publication Society of America. 1971.

Seigel, Robert A. "Conversion as Process." *Bamakom.* Vol. 1, No. 3. Spring 1974, p. 4 ff.

Shulman, Charles E. "Mixed Marriage, Conversion and Reality." *C.C.A. R. Journal.* January 1964. pp. 27-32.

Sklare, Marshall. "Intermarriage and Jewish Survival." *Commentary.* Vol. 3, 1970. p. 52 ff.

Stern, Malcolm. "Jewish Marriage and Intermarriage in the Federal Period (1776-1840)." *American Jewish Archives.* Vol. 19, November 1967.